HOW I'VE ACHIEVED
TRIPLE-DIGIT RETURNS
DAYTRADING . . . 4 HOURS A DAY

HOW I'VE ACHIEVED
TRIPLE-DIGIT RETURNS
DAYTRADING . . . 4 HOURS A DAY

by David Floyd

TradingMarkets™
PUBLISHING GROUP

ISBN: 0-9721229-4-X

Printed in the United States of America

The book was typeset in Palatino by Judy Brown.

Disclaimer

It should not be assumed that the methods, techniques, or indicators presented in this book will be profitable or that they will not result in losses. Past results are not necessarily indicative of future results. Examples in this book are for educational purposes only. The author, publishing firm, and any affiliates assume no responsibility for your trading results. This is not a solicitation of any order to buy or sell.

The NFA requires us to state that "HYPOTHETICAL OR SIMULATED PERFORMANCE RESULTS HAVE CERTAIN INHERENT LIMITATIONS. UNLIKE AN ACTUAL PERFORMANCE RECORD, SIMULATED RESULTS DO NOT REPRESENT ACTUAL TRADING. ALSO, SINCE THE TRADES HAVE NOT ACTUALLY BEEN EXECUTED, THE RESULTS MAY HAVE UNDER- OR OVERCOMPENSATED FOR THE IMPACT, IF ANY, OF CERTAIN MARKET FACTORS, SUCH AS LACK OF LIQUIDITY. SIMULATED TRADING PROGRAMS IN GENERAL ARE ALSO SUBJECT TO THE FACT THAT THEY ARE DESIGNED WITH THE BENEFIT OF HINDSIGHT. NO REPRESENTATION IS BEING MADE THAT ANY ACCOUNT WILL OR IS LIKELY TO ACHIEVE PROFITS OR LOSSES SIMILAR TO THOSE SHOWN."

I dedicate this book to my wife, Debbie, for tolerating my strange work hours and standing by me during the early years, when it was not really clear that I was going to make it as a trader.

To my wonderful son, Tyler, you are truly amazing.

And lastly, to my Mom and Dad. Without you, none of this would have been possible.

Contents

ACKNOWLEDGMENTS

This book has taken tremendous effort from many people. I especially want to thank Todd Gordon for his tireless efforts in helping me put together all of the graphics. This project would not have been completed without his assistance. Thanks to Todd and Bo Harvey for helping out when my schedule got a little tight. I want to thank Larry Connors and Eddie Kwong for giving me a chance, back in 2001. It has been a great experience.

HOW I'VE ACHIEVED TRIPLE-DIGIT RETURNS
DAYTRADING . . . 4 HOURS A DAY

INTRODUCTION

The Summer of 2002 was turning out to be a summer just like any other, in terms of trading—slow-motion price action, very little institutional participation, and most trading desks minimally staffed, as sun and sand took precedence over charts and quotes.

After nine years as a daytrader, I had come to expect little from summer trading. Sure, I would make money, but not "meaningful" money.

Summer mornings usually look something like this: There is some activity in the first hour or so; after that, I usually pack it up and head down to the marina or play some golf. That's not being lazy. It's being smart. Bottom line: Summers are not the best time for traders. (An exception I recall was August 1998—the Long-Term Capital Management crisis.)

Up until this time, the very analysts who had completely missed the bursting of the Nasdaq bubble were now confidently trumpeting a return to growth and prosperity, even as we were heading back to the post 9/11 lows of 944.74 in the S&P 500 index. All I remember hearing was profits this, growth that. I found it incredibly amusing but at the same time sad that the same people who are wrong 90% of the time kept coming back with more unrealistic predictions.

As a trader though, it was a mere distraction. Sure, I had my own opinions at the time, and they were not even close to what these so-called experts predicted, but that was not important. What was important was to trade the market based on the charts. And at the time, the charts were not looking too good. The market was slowly creeping back down to 944.74. A bear raid while the troops were out vacationing in the Hamptons. It was interesting to watch from the sidelines.

MY BEST FRIEND . . . *FEAR*

And then it happened. On July 10, the S&Ps cut through that "critical" 944.74 level like it wasn't even there. Suddenly, for the first time in many months, there was fear in the market. You could smell it, taste it and see it. Fear: a trader's best friend. This was a situation where investors who had had their heads in the sand suddenly looked up, panicked and sold as if their lives depended upon it.

While I was certainly not panicking, I was certainly more than willing to step up and do some serious selling myself. Heck, why be a party pooper? The only difference was that I was selling short.

And so it began. Suddenly, my trips with my wife Debbie and son Tyler to the marina were put on hold so I could play in the best trading environment I had seen since early 2000. The marina would be there when I was done.

Now, given that I had been through two similar periods before, I knew exactly what needed to be done:

1. Trade assertively, anticipate, but don't think too much.

2. Double, triple, and even quadruple my share size.

These periods do not come by all that often. Most of the year, traders make a living just like everyone else, grinding it out. But every so often, the money tree starts shaking, and you need to be there to catch the money before it falls to the ground.

During those two weeks, I made as much as I'd made so far for that year-to-date. I traded bell-to-bell most of the days and was completely exhausted by day's end. But it was beautiful. The days that followed were a string of 30- to 50-point down days in the S&P futures. The range intraday was insane. At the time, I mainly traded stocks like Citigroup and American International, while close colleagues in my office were having their way with Wal-Mart and Home Depot. We played right on the edge, but were always in control. If you let fear and greed get in the way, you were doomed.

Despite the fun and camaraderie, the mood on the desk was intense and the trading action required incredible focus.

For me, it really boiled down to one thing: *pinpointing and anticipating the exact times the S&Ps were about to make a powerful move up or down.* My eyes were glued to the 1-minute chart of the S&Ps while monitoring trades in the underlying stocks.

ONE TRADE I REMEMBER WELL . . .

The S&Ps pushed below support, bids were falling away in both the futures and the underlying stock. I was quick, but missed out occasionally. This time, I was fortunate. The futures were torpedoing to new lows on the day, and I shorted off a 4,000-share bid on Citibank at 33.40 that was sitting on Instinet.

The S&P futures were:

> *"843 bid 844 offer" with 100 cars (100 contracts) offered . . . then a moment later, "842 bid 843 offer," still 100 cars . . . and so it progressed down to 831.*

Meanwhile Citibank was starting its own torpedo dance. The stock immediately began to follow the S&Ps down. As the seconds ticked by, the market in New York went like this:

> *33.35 × 33.45 . . . 33.10 × 33.25 . . . 33 × 33.10 . . . and then 32.75 × 33*

And then the specialist gave me the sign to cover the short. If you have played this game long enough, you know it when you see it.

> *32 × 33 with 50,000 shares offered and only 1,000 on the bid.*

I did not even flinch, I immediately sent in my order:

> *"Buy 4,000 C at MARKET!"*

I sat there, licking my lips. I knew I had made the right call. The next trade went off at 32.50, almost a minute later. That is where . . .

> *. . . I was filled. $3,600 in less than 5 minutes. (This was one of the 40 or so trades I made that day. And during that three-week period, I made over 500 trades.)*

Immediately his market was:

> *32.75 × 33.25 now with 100,000 shares on the bid, and the S&Ps were on a ripper back up.*

Timing is everything in this business. He gave the signal and it was up to me to act. I did. I have ignored those subtle signals in the past, only to see a good trade turn into a scratch, or worse, a loser.

And so it continued for almost three weeks. The summer that I had written off awoke like I could never have imagined. I am waiting patiently for the next time the market decides to go on another roller coaster ride. It will probably be a couple of years, but I'll be waiting.

BACK TO THE ROUTINE OF MAKING A LIVING DAYTRADING . . .

Through times such as I have just described and through times considerably less exciting, I have daytraded professionally for nine years. At the time of writing (November 2002), I have had *only one losing month trading since 1998.*

In this book, I will teach you the strategy that has not only enabled me to produce this high level of consistent performance, but which has also enabled me to earn my entire livelihood daytrading stocks, both through the bull market of the late 1990s and well into the bear market of the early 2000s. This is the same strategy that I have successfully taught in one-on-one mentoring to dozens of students.

When I set out to write this book, I had one goal in mind:

> To teach my winning strategy in as simple a way as possible, to help people to achieve real results. That is because no matter how good a strategy is, trading for a living is one of the most difficult professions in the world. It takes the discipline of a Navy Seal and the emotional stamina of a heart surgeon.

> If you are serious about entering this profession, you can bet on one thing: You will have ample challenges and you don't need me to complicate your life by communicating my message poorly.

So I asked myself: "How can I make this more compelling and different from all the other daytrading books out there?" It did not take long to come up with the answer.

> **I want you to actually sit with me while I am trading.** Physically, we know that this is impossible while you are reading a book, but I want to give you as close an approximation as possible. I will not only show you step-by-step how I identify, plan, and act on trading setups, but I will also teach you from actual trades I've made, narrating precisely what is going on as each trade unfolds.

I want to emphasize that the examples I show you in this course are from real trades that I made. I will walk you through trades from beginning to end, providing you with the exact thought process that went into each buy and sell decision. This will enable you to see first hand how my strategies are applied in real-world trading.

HERE'S WHAT YOU'LL LEARN

This book is divided into two parts. Part I gives you the foundation for putting the odds in your favor and making the best use of my strategies. In Part II, you will learn the HVT strategy itself.

Part I: Putting the Odds in Your Favor When You Trade

Chapter 1 explains how High Velocity Trading (HVT) differs from other styles of trading. Learn the advantages you have as an HVT trader in quickly capturing high-probability trading opportunities.

Chapter 2 shows you how to trade for a living the HVT way, and how it enables you to earn a regular paycheck without the stress caused by unpredictable news events that jolt the stock market. And you don't have to worry about whether we're in a bear or bull market.

Chapter 3 teaches you how to get a powerful edge by trading NYSE stocks. Learn the personality of NYSE stocks and use that to your advantage. Also, find out how the majority of daytraders unknowingly lose an important edge by focusing on Nasdaq stocks.

Part II: Trading Successfully the HVT Way

Chapter 4 shows how to use stock index futures as an early-warning "radar screen," alerting you to incoming HVT trading opportunities. Once you understand the relationship between stocks and futures, you will be able to catch trends the way a surfer catches waves.

Chapter 5 explains how to identify strong intraday trends and focus on entering when the risk is lowest and where the probability of making money is the highest.

Chapter 6 shows you the proper way to use stochastics to keep you in high-probability trades and detect high-risk trades that you should be staying out of. Stochastics is a widely misused indicator, but I will teach you to use it properly.

Chapter 7 leads you out onto the trading battlefield as you learn how trading setups form on 1-minute charts . . . and most importantly, how to identify them quickly.

Chapter 8 explains how to use tick charts to pinpoint your entries and exits at precisely the right moment—at the best price. You will learn to time your entries down to the millisecond.

Chapter 9 shows how to use 5-minute charts as an indicator. While most conventional daytraders use them to identify trading setups, I will show you how to use them as a filtering mechanism to tell you what setups to stay out of, a nice ploy that keeps you many steps ahead of the crowd.

Chapter 10 illustrates the most efficient approach I have found for keeping all the most critical information within my field of vision during the trading day. You will learn my complete screen layout, a component as important to my success as any strategy I will teach you.

Chapter 11 shows you everything you need to know about the Level I quote screen to place buy and sell orders at lightning speed. This is important because in HVT, the speed at which you are able to move in and out of trades can mean the difference between profit and loss.

Chapter 12 details how you can successfully short stock in fast-moving markets in spite of the "uptick rule." You will learn to do this using bullets and conversions.

Chapter 13 shows you how to prepare yourself each day before the market opens, to take immediate advantage of key support and resistance levels set to influence market action through the course of the trading day.

Chapter 14 teaches you how to combine all the indicators and patterns I have taught you up until this point and use them to identify key HVT trading setups. I will reveal my thought process and trading logic, from the stalking stage to entry and exit. Through these examples, you will learn how to use the same strategies in a variety of different market conditions.

Chapter 15 covers perhaps the most important topic of all—money management and psychology. No matter how good your odds become when you use HVT, you must always use stop losses. In this chapter, I will teach you how to trade with total discipline and focus, so that you will not get knocked out of the game. Plus, I will teach you how to avoid burnout by taking time off.

PART ONE

Putting The Odds In Your Favor When You Trade

CHAPTER ONE

What Is High Velocity Trading (HVT)?

I make my living daytrading 4 hours a day. Here's how . . .

The name "High Velocity Trading" (HVT) itself roughly describes what I do for a living. I make fast trading decisions dozens of times a day and enter trades that are, compared with other trading styles, relatively short in duration.

I define HVT as follows:

> HVT is the process whereby you make several trades intraday, catching the short-term trend of a stock. The entry is triggered by the price action of the S&P 500 futures.

In the coming chapters I will teach you exactly how this is done by walking you through many examples. For now, I will briefly summarize my strategy from beginning to end:

The HVT Checklist:

- ☑ Determine the trend in the S&P Futures on a 1-minute chart.

- ☑ Look for the same trend in the individual stock that you are looking to trade on a 1-minute chart.

- ☑ Identify pullbacks within the trend in stochastics in both the S&P futures and the stock.

- ☑ Identify pullbacks within the price trend in both S&P futures and the stock.

- ☑ Identify that a resumption of the trend in S&P futures and stochastics is beginning.

- ☑ Enter limit order in stock on "market burst pattern" in S&P Futures tick charts.

- ☑ Watch for the momentum to slow down in stochastics and the tick chart.

- ☑ Exit at market on first sign of weakening of the trend as indicated by the tick chart.

All of the above is built on a solid foundation of strict discipline and money management. In case you are wondering, the reason you do not see stop placement as one of the items in the checklist is that actual stop-loss orders are not possible because of the fast pace of HVT. However, keeping losses small is built into HVT through its exit strategy, based on patterns in the tick chart. I will explain this in Chapter 8.

WHY DID I BECOME A HIGH-VELOCITY TRADER?

I'll say it now and I'll probably say it again several times in this book:

I hate to lose. I'm no different than anyone else.

So I developed a style of trading that would not only enable me to trade for a living, but also fit my personality.

In my opinion, HVT is the best approach for achieving consistent returns over a long period of time. Consistent and long-term profitability, coupled with a **relatively high ratio of 70% to 90% winning trades,** makes HVT a style of trading that is perfectly suited to my needs.

I developed this approach in the early 1990s and it continues to work well for me to this very day.

And now, I want to share this knowledge with the rest of world. And I suspect there are many who will listen. Any time I describe to people exactly what I do, and that I am able to consistently achieve a high percentage of winning trades, it touches a nerve. They want to learn!

Advantages

There are many reasons why you should seriously consider using this approach:

1. **No overnight risk.** Since you will buy and sell stocks all on the same day, you will always end the day completely out of the market. This protects you from unpleasant overnight surprises that cause a stock to gap down or up at the next day's open.

2. **High probability on a per trade basis—a 70% win/loss ratio is not uncommon among experienced HVT traders.** This alone offers a tremendous psychological edge vs. the 30% win/loss ratio associated with other trading methodologies.

3. **Consistent returns with minimal equity draw-downs.** I will teach you how to enter at points where the probability is highest that a stock will move immediately in your favor. If a stock moves against you, you will know instantly that you are wrong. Operating this way allows you to set tight stops and keep your risk on each trade very small.

4. **Little to no research each night to prepare for next day.** Unlike the majority of short-term traders, you won't need to spend hours and hours researching which stocks you'll be focusing on the next day. That's because I will show you how to trade the same stocks every day.

5. **The strategy you will learn is applicable to the daily and monthly time frame.** While my main focus is intraday trading, once you have learned it, you will find it applicable to longer-term time frames.

6. **You can earn enough to make a living trading fewer than 4 hours a day.** I trade for about 4 hours per day, morning session from 6:30–8:30 A.M. PST and afternoon session from 11:00–1:00 P.M. PST.

Disadvantages

There are certain important trade-offs to consider:

1. **You will need to give up the opportunity for bigger gains achieved with longer time frames.** Many times you will see that, after having exited a profitable trade according to my trading rules, a stock will just keep going. If you want the high ratio of winning to losing trades that HVT offers you, you will have to live with the prospect that you will sometimes only carve out a portion of a big move.

2. **HVT requires immense concentration and being in front of your computer during trading hours.** In HVT, you must maintain a sharp focus constantly, to ensure survival . . . and to make money.

3. **You need incredible discipline and money management.** Being a successful trader requires being able to execute money management rules flawlessly. If a trade is not going as it should, you must exit immediately without hesitation. Many people cannot bring themselves to do this.

4. **At times it can be mundane when markets are dull.** Sometimes hours can go by in which no trading opportunities arise. You have to live with that and yet constantly stay on your toes and be alert for setups when the action picks up.

HVT IS NOT WHAT YOU MAY THINK . . .

I am amazed at the number of people who watch me trade and, seeing how rapidly I get in and out of trades, conclude that I am a "scalper." Because people get this first impression, I am going to spend some time using the contrast between "scalping" and HVT to help you understand the differences and how HVT skews the odds in my favor.

Scalping refers to a style of trading that is far less structured and more prone to random outcomes than what I do in HVT.

Let me give you a brief example of what scalpers do. Don't worry if you do not understand all the technicalities of scalping. I am merely using this to illustrate how HVT is better.

Scalping, based on the classic definition, is where one buys stock on the bid with the intention of immediately exiting on the offer for a quick profit on the spread between the Bid and Ask. The classic example of a scalper is described in the following transaction:

John evaluates the spread on DNA (Genentech). It is currently showing a market of:

Symbol	Bid/Ask	Bid/Ask Size*
DNA	47.65 × 47.70	10 × 55

*(Bid and offer size are always shown in 100s)

John thinks that with a market of 47.65 × 47.70, 1,000 shares on the bid and 5,500 on the offer, represented as 10 × 55, DNA won't go down any further from here. He enters an order to buy 500 shares at 47.65. Once that order is entered, the bid size should reflect John's bid of 500 shares.

Here is what happens immediately after John enters his order.

Symbol	Bid/Ask	Bid/Ask Size
DNA	47.65 × 47.70	(15) × 55

John's 500 shares go in the bid queue and I've circled the bid size to illustrate.

As you can see, John at this point is last in line to be filled at 47.65 unless other stock shows up on the bid, which is what he anticipates. If he is filled, he will immediately offer it out at 47.70 and wait for his order to be filled, again at the back of the line, thereby pocketing .05 cents for his efforts.

The mere fact that John wants to buy on the bid is a major drawback to this methodology. In order for him to get filled, he is hoping that someone will sell the stock at 47.65, which may or may not happen. Plus, he is making the assumption that even if he gets his stock at 47.65, the sellers will evaporate and then suddenly he'll be able to sell his stock at 47.70, for a quick profit.

Do you see the flaws in this logic?

There are too many empty assumptions. John is thinking he knows exactly where the market is going to turn. Perhaps he does, but more times than not, most of us cannot pick turning points that accurately. What happens if more sellers show up, and the bid then becomes 47.60, and they hit that bid also? Secondly, he is also saying to himself that if the stock does go up, it will only go up 5 cents. Again, how does he know that, and what happens if it goes up another 20 cents after he is filled? The risk/reward dynamics on this trade are very poor. You get the point.

HERE IS HOW THE HVT TRADER OPERATES

I am not completely dismissing the scalping strategy, as I am aware of many people who do this day in and day out and do quite well.

But HVT allows me to stack the odds in my favor. This leads to the lower risk/higher payoff *every time I get into a trade*. An example will help clarify this:

Let's say that Dave, an HVT trader, has valid technical evidence that DNA is going higher and that the market is the same as in John's example. Dave would much rather wait until the market indeed confirms that it is going higher and then buy the offer along with all the other buyers that may be inclined to get in on the beginning of the rally.

What you are doing in this scenario is aligning your position with the trend of the market, as opposed to buying into selling pressure, in the hopes that the flood of buyers is right around the corner.

Assuming Dave is correct about the direction of DNA, the scenario may unfold as follows: Dave buys 1000 shares at 47.70. Instead of standing in line with all the other bids, his buy order gets executed immediately.

Below, I have circled his trade.

Symbol	Bid/Ask	Bid/Ask Size	Last Trade
DNA	47.65 × 47.70	10 × 55	⑩

The market now becomes:

Symbol	Bid/Ask	Bid/Ask Size	Last Trade
DNA	47.65 × 47.70	10 × 45	

Let's assume that two more trades occur at 47.70, one for 3,000 shares and one for 1,500 shares. Your quotes would look like this after each trade.

Symbol	Bid/Ask	Bid/Ask Size	Last Trade
DNA	47.65 × 47.70	10 × 15	30

Symbol	Bid/Ask	Bid/Ask Size	Last Trade
DNA	47.70 × 47.80	20 × 30	15

Because Dave has done his homework, he is correct in his anticipation that the market will move higher. The price at which Dave bought the stock is now the bid. In theory if he is wrong on the trade, he can simply sell at market and get out at 47.70 for a "scratch" on the trade.

Contrast this with scalping. You might have bought the stock at 47.65 and then the market becomes 47.55 × 47.65. Immediately you will find yourself in the hole!

HVT IS FAST, LIKE SCALPING, BUT TRADING OFF TRENDS, NOT SPREADS

So, even though people conclude that I am a scalper because they see fast, precision entries and exits, in reality I am doing the opposite of scalping.

I buy on the offer and sell on the bid, much like the rest of the world.

I am not interested in trying to get "cute" by playing the spread. Unless you have a stock that moves very little such as a utility, scalping is a much lower-probability strategy than HVT.

But I only do this because I know the odds are favorable that the stock I'm in will move in my favor. This depends upon a combination of elements that really defines what HVT is. Every one of the following components of HVT works to better your odds. In HVT trading, you . . .

- Make several trades in a single day, based upon the price action of the S&P 500 futures.

- Trade the same small group of stocks every day.

- Trade only with the trend and never against.

- Usually enter trades at key support or resistance levels.

- Take profits fast in order to minimize risk.

These factors and others that I will teach you, enable me to begin each trading day with the expectation of making money. Rarely am I disappointed.

CHAPTER TWO

How I Trade For a Living . . . One Day at a Time

Here are two "big picture" rules that will give you the best chance of long-term success as a daytrader . . .

I want you to step back for a moment and look at the big picture. **What really is required to make a living trading using HVT?** I want you to focus on this now so that you will understand the utter seriousness of what I am about to teach you.

You see, I trade professionally. At the risk of sounding redundant, I make my living as a trader. *To me, trading successfully is almost a matter of life and death.*

So whether you intend to trade full-time professionally, or part-time to supplement your regular income, I believe you must look at trading in this way in order to have the intensity of focus that is essential in this business. It is not a hobby. It is not recreation. Once you start treating it as hobby or a fun pastime, you will let your guard down. For most people, that is all that needs to happen for them to be knocked out of business permanently. That is how life and death is.

TWO SIMPLE WAYS TO MAXIMIZE YOUR LONGEVITY AS A TRADER

In this section, I want to explain two rules which, if followed religiously, will give you the best chance of success as a daytrader.

#1: Do Everything Possible to Make Money Every Day

To daytrade professionally, it is important to make money—if possible—every single day. That may seem obvious. But let me illustrate how important it is to me and those who depend on me.

> I sweep my trading account back to a particular dollar amount every two weeks or sometimes once a month. This money is then set aside in my checking account, less Uncle Sam's cut, which I pay quarterly. This amount is then disbursed to my various creditors: mortgage, car and boat payments, groceries, etc. The remainder goes directly into my savings account at the local discount brokerage to be used from an investing/longer-term trading perspective.

Why do I tell you this? Simple. Trading is my job, so naturally my goal is to make money every single day, leading to my bi-weekly pay check just like every other American.

While of course it is virtually impossible to make money every day, I have, over the years—by necessity—averaged roughly an 85% profitability ratio, day to day. Not too bad. This ratio is what allows me to create a consistent revenue stream from which to live.

The moral of my story? Trade as though your life depended on it.

#2: Go Home Every Day Flat!

Knowing in the back of my mind that trading is what pays my bills allows me to overcome one constant temptation: holding positions overnight. In the world of trading and investing, holding stock positions overnight is what the vast majority of people in the world do. But I avoid it like the plague and doing the same is an essential policy for you to follow as an HVT trader.

Let me tell you what would happen if I suddenly started taking stocks home overnight in my trading account. There are three possible outcomes:

1. Large equity swings

2. Greater total return

3. Lower total return

Any benefit you might get from number 2, is far outweighed by larger equity swings. I know this may sound remedial and repetitive but it is so important. I am not telling you not to invest or swing trade. What I am saying is that you need to have a separate brokerage account for HVT trading. Never co-mingle the money. While your equity curve in an investment account will look like an EKG from time to time, the **plot of a successful trader's account should be a steady rise to the right. Period**.

The Six Top Valid Reasons Not to Do Overnight Trades in Your HVT Daytrading Account

- Overnight risk

- No mental baggage when day is done, focus on other things

- No need to work out of a hole on a news bomb or overnight political/economic bombshell

- When you come in in the morning, you can focus on trading, not damage control

- Overnight exposes you to 50/50 risk reward, whereas HVT can achieve 70% success on trade-by-trade basis

- Overnight positions take control out of your hands

CHAPTER THREE

The Stocks That Give You an Edge *Before You Even Start Trading*

In the late 90s, "they" said I was crazy for trading NYSE stocks instead of Nasdaq stocks. Here's why they should have listened . . .

I n this chapter I will teach you some concepts which, if you have already been trading for a while, will sound rather unconventional. But what I teach you here is an essential part of what has enabled me to be successful all these years.

NYSE OR NASDAQ?

I trade NYSE stocks almost exclusively. And I have been doing so even during the late 90s when everybody was making "easy money" trading Nasdaq stocks. Yes, people did question my sanity behind my back. But to this very day, in the midst of one of the worst bear markets in history and the Nasdaq having lost its glamour, I remain happy and content making steady money from those "boring NYSE stocks."

As a trader who is clearly in the minority on this issue, I have a lot of explaining to do.

I won't argue for a moment that Nasdaq stocks DO exhibit more volatility intraday, but capturing those moves is easier said than done.

Secondly, trying to get filled on large orders, say 2,000 shares and above, is a bit tricky as well. The Nasdaq simply does not have the depth at each price level that the NYSE does.

But that is only a sliver of the long list of Nasdaq disadvantages in my opinion. The mere structure of the Nasdaq market is fragmented, meaning the order flow is not centralized. Practically nobody in this business realizes what an important issue that is.

NYSE stocks have a centralized order book that is controlled by one individual, the specialist. Therefore, you have a much better chance of _learning the personality traits_ of that individual, thereby giving you a slight but important edge. I know this from my own experience, and that of other traders who work closely with me. When large orders hit the specialist's book _he will do certain things the same way time and time again._ It is predictable and you can use this to your advantage.

Let me now go over the list of advantages that you will have trading NYSE as opposed to Nasdaq stocks. Let's simply look at the contrast:

- **The NYSE has greater depth than the Nasdaq on bid/asks.** That means that there is a greater likelihood that your order will get filled _at the price you want,_ even if you are trading large size.

- **The NYSE offers you a more orderly market.** Some people look at intraday charts of the Nasdaq and drool when they see the wide price swings. They see themselves playing these moves and making money from them. That is really, in my opinion, a delusion because much of that movement is random, unpredictable noise. What good are these kinds of large swings, if trading them is like playing slot machines in Las Vegas? If you are less interested in excitement, and more interested in making money, _NYSE stocks offer you better trending behavior and better predictability._

- **The NYSE provides you with a centralized market in which order flow is controlled by the specialist.** This allows you to *learn the personality of a stock* which aids your ability to anticipate future price behavior beyond just what you see technically.

- **The NYSE has large institutional participation** which gives you *superior liquidity* and lessens the likelihood of abrupt swings that can wipe out a position.

- **In my experience, you can trade NYSE with *lower transaction costs.*** That depends on your individual broker, but I believe if you do your homework, you will find this to be the case.

LIMIT YOUR FOCUS TO MAXIMIZE YOUR PROFITS

I've told you what market to focus on. Now let me tell you what stocks you should be trading. One of the most unique aspects of HVT is that you will be limiting your trading to the same small group of NYSE stocks, day after day, week after week. This is consistent with the philosophy of HVT, which is to maximize the odds of success.

If you are already a daytrader, chances are that you come from a different school of thought. Every night, you spend several hours researching your "hit list" for the next day. Every day, it's a different list of stocks that you've identified as being in the barn-burning industry groups, having the right patterns, and which are exhibiting extreme relative strength readings. All of this, as the reasoning goes, is to increase the odds of success.

This approach works for many traders, but it's not for HVT traders. It is very easy to get sidetracked by external factors, especially in the market. One moment you are trading XYZ, the next you are trading ABC, because your friend or a report on CNBC told you about it. **This lack of continuity is the poison that eliminates traders.**

An observation will help clarify this:

Walk on to the floor of the NYSE, CME or even Merrill Lynch's trading desk and ask individuals what they do. Ninety-nine percent of the people will give you an answer that indicates they specialize in one particular area or stock. Lewis Borsellino, a 20-year veteran of the S&P pit, does not jump from the S&P pit over to the soybean pit because he hears the action is "hot" over there. No, he stays and focuses on what he knows, the inner workings of the S&P pit, something the casual observer or armchair trader could never figure out. Same goes for the specialist of IBM's stock: He knows all the floor brokers that work orders for IBM regularly and he probably even has a pretty good idea of what to expect for order flow under different scenarios, and adjusts his trading approach accordingly. Remember, many specialists trade upwards of a third of the daily volume for their own book, in addition to matching up orders. You need to know what that specialist is thinking.

You see where I am going with this? The focus and discipline you get from limiting the number of stocks you trade, will dramatically increase your odds of success.

There were many people I spoke with during the big bubble of 1999 and 2000 at presentations I made. These individuals basically thought I was a loony for not trading the "hot" Internet stocks.

> My answer was simply: "I trade what I know, and until it does not work anymore, I have no intention of abandoning my approach."

You see, the 1999 and 2000 period left many newer traders with false confidence about their actual abilities as traders. Let's be honest. It was not real difficult to simply latch onto a move and pull a few hundred or thousand bucks out, with little or no effort. The problem was that these individuals were never defining their strategy. Most could not answer clearly why or how they did their trades. Once the bubble burst, many were left scratching their heads. I wonder where those traders are now? You know the answer.

Every approach, no matter how robust, will have periods where it is not yielding results. The important thing is not to walk away and start dabbling elsewhere. It is like most things in life, it goes through cycles. Your job is to minimize equity drawdowns during those down cycles.

> You need to focus on producing a steady, reliable revenue stream from trading by always targeting situations where you know the odds are in your favor. With HVT, I have already done my "homework" once and for all times to come. It's all the research that I put into testing and honing the HVT strategy several years ago and which I apply over and over again each day on the same stocks. Same familiar faces. The variables are all known every day I trade. My assessment of the odds on any trade is about as accurate as it can be.

I don't have to redo my homework every night with "nightly research" and introduce new, unknown and potentially dangerous variables.

I have been trading virtually the same way for nine years now. I survived and thrived during the bubble years and continued to trade successfully after the bubble burst. Focus and discipline tend to yield wonderful results. Yes, I have made adjustments, but none so radical that it has changed my overall approach.

So what does this mean for you?

 Find between 3 and 5 stocks. Find stocks that belong to different sectors, and simply watch them and trade them, day in and day out.

Remember, the specialists and market makers do have an advantage. They see all the order flow, and act accordingly. They are human beings though. And successful humans tend to do what? They do what works over and over again. It is a safe assumption that the specialist in AOL will do certain things to his book to accommodate large orders. The same can be said regarding floor brokers, as they will do certain things in order to move large blocks of stock. It is this simple fact that allows you to gain an edge. Is this the glamorous approach to trading? Hardly, but it is the right approach. I do not trade to drop names at cocktail parties of all the story stocks I traded that day.

I trade to win.

HOW TO SELECT THE STOCKS YOU WILL TRADE EACH DAY

As amazing as it may sound, between 1999 and 2000, 85% of my income came from 2–3 stocks. I traded them day in, and day out. There were days where I was 1% of the volume in a stock. This, if nothing else, should convince you of the importance of focus.

Here is a list which gives you the characteristics and requirements of the stocks I trade.

The list below simply illustrates minimum requirements.

- Daily Volume > 1,000,000 shares

- Average daily price range > $1.50

- A price > $20

- Stock is highly correlated with the S&P futures

If you did do this AIQ match market would get you the stocks

The Usual Suspects

These are examples of the stocks that I trade on the NYSE

- IBM

- TXN

- HD

- C

- WMT

- GE

PART TWO

Trading Successfully The HVT Way

CHAPTER FOUR

The Relationship Between Stocks and Futures . . . the *Basis for HVT*

> **How you can buy stocks right at the beginning of explosive moves . . .**

Understanding how stocks move in conjunction with the S&P and Nasdaq Futures is the cornerstone for your proper advancement. I am going to teach you how movement in the futures leads stock movement by a split second and how you can take advantage of this.

Some of the concepts may be arcane or even confusing. I go into them only as a way of showing you the big picture. The bottom line, regardless of the dynamics behind the scenes, is:

> Stocks that make good daytrading vehicles *move in tandem with the futures*. Period.

Here's what you need to know when it comes down to the relationship between the futures and individual stocks. I'll let the pictures tell the story.

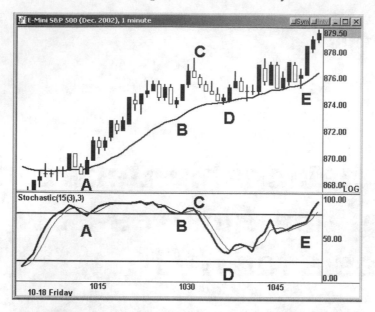

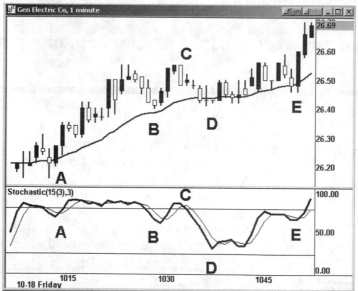

Figure 4-1

The chart on the top is a 1-minute chart of the S&P E-mini futures. The one below it is a 1-minute chart of GE for the same corresponding time period.

Notice any similarities between them? If not, look at each individual letter in the top chart vs. its corresponding letter in the chart below. In terms of time, stochastics and price action, they are identical.

What you cannot see in these charts, as will be shown later, is that the futures have a slight lead time over the underlying stock. That is why using the futures as your leading indicator is so vitally important.

I often get the question: If you focus on the futures so much, why not just trade them? It is a great question. The reason is simple: If the futures lead stocks, **don't you want to trade a vehicle that has a split-second lag time built into it?**

Executing a futures trade based on the same parameters amounts to your placing the trade once the futures make that move. Essentially, you are chasing the entry point. Contrast that with stocks. You can potentially be the first one on board BEFORE they move, IF you analyze the futures properly.

So why do stocks have this correlation with the S&P and Nasdaq futures? A brief explanation of the concept of arbitrage and fair value will shed some light.

WHERE THAT SPLIT-SECOND LAG TIME COMES FROM

A futures contract, as we all know, is nothing more than a perceived value of an asset (corn, oil, bonds or in some cases, a basket of stocks) at a predetermined point in the future (settlement/expiration date). As the value of that contract fluctuates, so does the value of the underlying asset that makes up the futures contract.

> An example: If a September 2002 futures contract for a barrel of oil is trading at $18 and the underlying asset (the barrel of oil) is trading at $17.50, you would assume that as the value of the future rises, the oil should also rise, but only to the point where it maintains the 50 cent spread, or what is called "Fair Value." Where that spread gets out of whack is when you get additional buying and selling pressure, (buy and sell programs in the S&P futures).

If you are a trader looking at a 1-minute chart of the Sept. Oil Futures and you notice it spike up 20 cents, you can make a pretty safe assumption that the actual asset will not be far behind in its move to re-establish fair value/parity.

The exact same scenario plays out every day in the S&P and Nasdaq pits in Chicago. This, my friends, is the driver of HVT.

Now in the pits you have a lot of traders (some are locals or market makers) who are there to facilitate order flow from the large institutions, essentially taking the other sides of their trades. Locals have two options after filling a buy or a sell order. They may find that the market turns in their direction or the market begins to go against them. Let's assume that a local just bought 100 S&P contracts from the Morgan Stanley broker. He is now long the market, but let's assume that the Morgan Stanley broker has more to sell and by doing so, pushes the futures through a support level and . . .

. . . the market begins to tank. **I need to emphasize this point, so I'll say it again. The futures are moving lower.**

What does the local do? One of two things. Perhaps he was already short and the trade with Morgan Stanley simply flattened him out. Or perhaps he is in a bit of trouble now. What can he do? One solution is that he can sell stock against his 100 contract position as a hedge. Whatever that dollar amount is will be executed. Now it is impossible to buy all 500 stocks, so what arbitragers do is simply buy a basket of the 20 largest stocks, the Major Market Index, XMI—these are stocks like GE, MSFT, IBM, etc. By entering these orders, it further precipitates the drop in the underlying stocks.

Now the stocks in that basket of sells are getting pushed lower.

Notice that action in the stocks was precipitated *after* the action in the futures. This is the slight time lag I was telling you about.

Simultaneously, you have arbitragers either in the pit or off the floor, taking advantage of the mis-pricing that occurs as the futures and underlying stock get away from fair value. They too will be selling stock and buying futures to lock in risk-free profits. It is this action, day in and day out, which makes HVT possible.

Eventually, the relationship between the futures and the stock needs to come back to parity. Think of Fair Value as a rubber band. In its normal state, there is no tension on the rubber band. But if you put the band on each of your index fingers and move your left hand to the left, while holding your right hand steady, you are adding stress. The minute you release the band from your left hand, the band returns to its normal state. The same concept applies if you were to pull with your right hand. When the value of the S&P 500 Index moves too far to either side of its FV, eventually FV must be reached again. This is done via arbitrage. While the concept of arbitrage is not important here, it is important to know that when the index is lower than FV or higher than FV, it usually triggers buy and sell programs.

Historically, this high degree of correlation has always existed, and I see no reason for it to vanish.

The real goal however is not necessarily to fixate on buy and sell programs, but rather to understand the dynamics of why stocks move in tandem with the futures.

Starting in the next chapter and throughout the rest of this book, I will show you exactly how to successfully use this relationship in HVT.

CHAPTER FIVE

How to Identify the "Real" Trend in the 1-Minute Universe

The most scientific way I know to determine the direction of a trend . . .

I cannot emphasize enough the importance of trading with the trend. So paramount is its importance that on days **when there is no discernable trend, I simply do not trade.**

You and I are just not smart enough to call turning points, to the penny. So, rather than agonizing about where the stock may turn, let the overall market and price action in the stock be your guide. Trust me, it is far more advantageous. I trade this way simply because I do not like to lose. I want every possible "edge" in my favor before I execute a trade.

Remember this: You will not go broke taking profits! You need to get yourself to a level of understanding about the market where you are exiting long positions towards overbought areas, and covering shorts at oversold areas.

At no point in this book will I discuss buying sell-offs in downtrends or shorting rallies in up trends.

I know what you are saying,

"I bought this book for you to tell me to trade with the trend?"

That's right, for three reasons:

1. Most people don't actually know how a trend is defined. Every trading style has its own definitions and there are quirks as to how one defines it.

2. Most people have a nasty tendency, even if they know what the trend is, to completely ignore it and take trades that buck the trend. This is one of the major reasons even seasoned traders give money back unnecessarily.

3. Some traders are influenced when they see big price changes. But the trend is not defined by the net change on the stock or futures for the day. It is very common to have the futures up 10 points on the day but with the immediate trend being down. Conversely, if the futures are down 15 points on the day, it is very common to be trading in an up-trend at some point during the day.

HOW TO CORRECTLY DETERMINE THE TREND IN THE 1-MINUTE UNIVERSE

As I watch the market I am continually evaluating and reevaluating the trend and the strength of the trend. It is not easy to do this by purely eyeballing price action. So I came up with a simple way to remove some of the subjectivity. Before I show you this, let's review how most people analyze trends.

Copyright © 2002 Quote LLC. All rights reserved. The information set forth in this screen shot is historical data only, and not current information.

Figure 5-1

If you take a look at this chart, you will notice that it had a very nice trend over the final hour of trading, from 13:45 to 14:30. One can make the argument that you would have accomplished a lot more by simply staying short for the whole move. That brings up an interesting point. It is very easy to look at a chart after the fact and read it left to right. It seems so obvious, doesn't it? But take a sheet of paper, cover up all the price action and then move the paper bar-by-bar to the right. What goes through your mind? It probably is not as crystal clear that the downtrend will continue. The advantage of HVT is that its whole basis is trading "in the now." We are not trying to make lofty predictions of what may happen in the next few minutes. If you get out of the trade, you can always get back in, if the opportunity presents itself.

HOW TO CORRECTLY DETERMINE THE TREND IN THE 1-MINUTE UNIVERSE

For the purposes of this book I will only define the trend as it relates to the 1-minute chart, PERIOD. I am not concerned what the trend is on a 5-minute, hourly or daily chart.

Let's take a look at the following charts. They are simply depictions of a 20-period exponential moving average on 1-minute charts. I have left out the price bars on purpose.

What is the trend on these two charts?

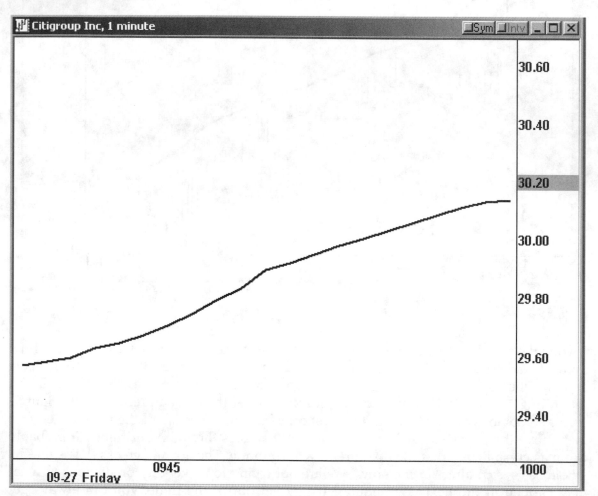

Figure 5-2

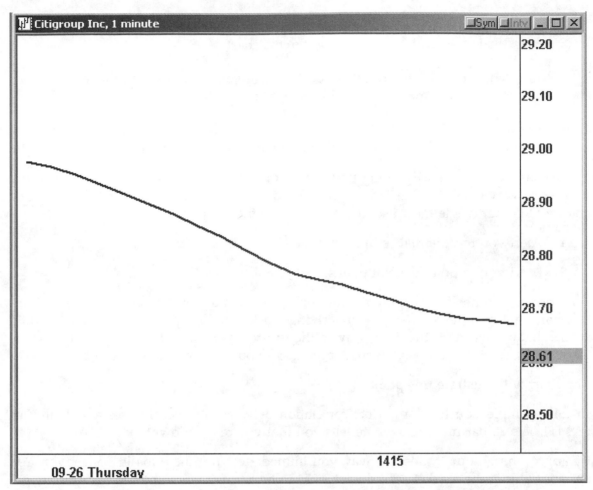

Figure 5-3

I suspect all of you answered correctly. As Dave Landry (author of *Dave Landry on Swing Trading*) likes to say, an uptrend is where the price action is going from the lower left to the upper right of the chart. A downtrend is where the price action is going from the upper left to the lower right of the chart. I use a slightly different approach that is specifically designed to remove the noise that would otherwise lead me astray in the time frame I trade in.

- The trend is defined by the slope of the 20-period moving average on the 1-minute chart.

- An uptrend is where the 20-period moving average on the 1-minute chart is going from the lower left to the upper right of the chart.

- A downtrend is where the 20-period moving average on the 1-minute chart is going from the upper left to the lower right of the chart.

Later in this chapter, I will show you some instances where it is very easy to confuse price action with trend. But for now, let's explore this concept a bit more.

Given that we are primarily doing trades in a rapid-fire manner, and are not attempting to forecast very far into the future—5 minutes at most—it makes sense that the 1-minute chart will be our single most useful tool. It will do the following:

1. Alert you to potential setups (entries)

2. Alert you to potential exit points

As a result, you need to display a minimum of at least a 1-minute chart of the S&P futures and a 1-minute chart of the underlying stock. Obviously, you want to be trading stocks that are trending the same way as the futures, as a way of simplifying the whole learning process. As you become more advanced, you can explore other tactics.

The chart will illustrate this point.

In this example you have a perfect correlation between the S&P futures and Wal-Mart (WMT). The 20-bar moving average tells you that you're in a downtrend.

By approaching your trades this way, you immediately put the odds in your favor: You are not fighting the market. You do not want to be a buyer when the S&P futures are going down and you do not want to be a seller when the S&P futures are going up.

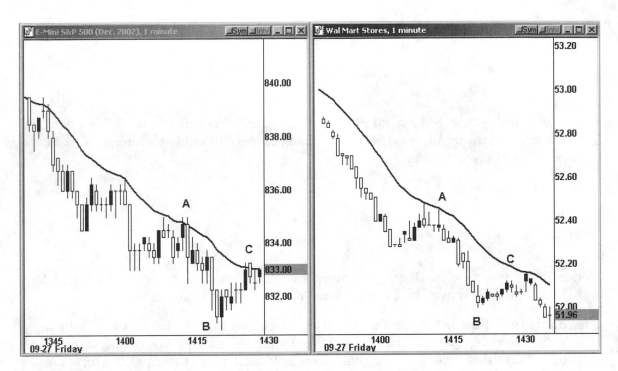

Figure 5-4

Take a look at the chart of General Electric (GE). I think it is safe to say at this point that it is clearly in an up-trend as noted by the rising 20-period moving average. Next notice the price range between letters:

> A to B and B to C

as well as . . .

> D to E and E to F.

Notice anything about the distance between the moves that went with the trend (A to B and D to E) and the moves that went against the trend (B to C and E to F)?

The counter-trend moves are less than half the price range on the up moves. That simple observation alone speaks volumes. You are reducing your range of possible entries and exits by 50%. In this case, assuming you were able to sell short right at the top of Point B which is $24.70 and cover at the bottom, $24.59 (Point C), you would have made 10 cents. But how realistic is that? It is not. When you take into consideration slippage, it is not difficult to see why *bucking the trend is a fool's bet*.

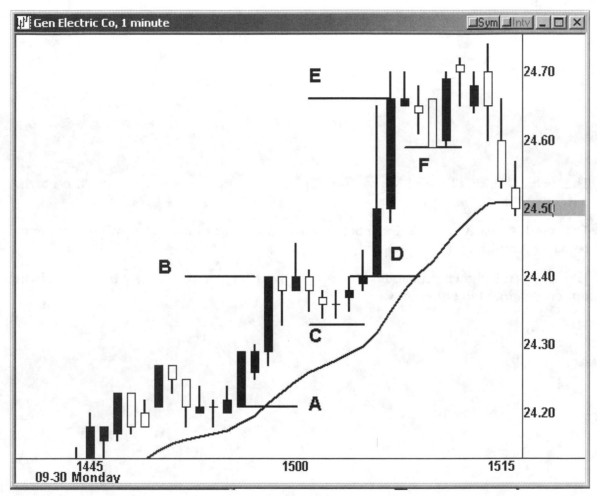

Figure 5-5

The next chart, this time of Microsoft (MSFT), shows the same type of scenario playing out.

The trend is clearly up, the range between B and C is small relative to what is exhibited between A and B and C and D.

The safer and higher probability trade is to wait for the pullback within the existing uptrend and go long at Point C.

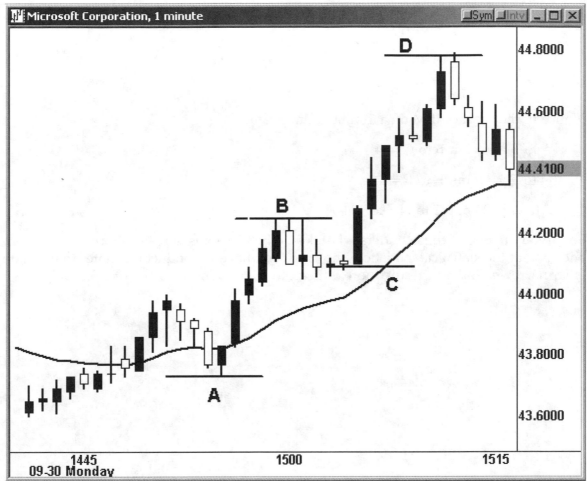

Figure 5-6

Notice in the chart of IBM on a 1-minute time frame:

A to B = .65 but B to C = .4

D to E = .39 but E to F = .28

F to G = .36 but G to H = .27

So, if you are one of those traders who likes to buy bottoms and sell short tops, go back and look at the statistical evidence. The range you have to conduct a counter trend trade is far narrower and as a result, more difficult to maneuver in and out of effectively.

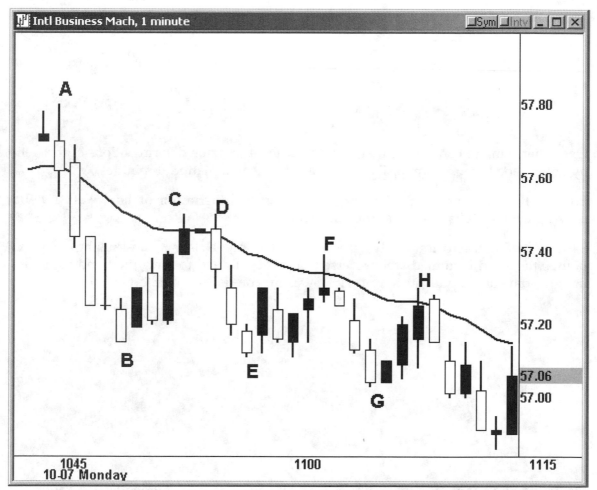

Figure 5-7

One other thing to consider is that you do not want to make determinations of the trend by going too far back in time. The trend can change in a matter of minutes.

Look at this chart of the S&P Futures. **It is a good illustration of how well a 20-bar moving average tells you what the real trend is.**

Despite having a ferocious rally up from 11 A.M. until 11:14 A.M. and taking on 7 S&P points, the trend is immediately reversed. If you continued to view the trend as up and bought some of the pullbacks from 11:30 A.M. on, you did not fare too well.

Flexibility and adaptation in a spilt second will pay you many dividends as a trader.

Keep it simple; trade with the trend as defined by the 20-period moving average.

Figure 5-8

CHAPTER SIX

How to Improve Your Odds on Every Trade, with Stochastics

A powerful way to use this much misused indicator . . .

Over the years, I have come to rely on stochastics for one very simple purpose: to keep me out of low-probability trades. Stochastics are of course, a lagging indicator, and if used as a timing vehicle, would be woefully inadequate in the context of HVT.

Despite that limitation, they are excellent at identifying areas of over-bought and oversold conditions. Any measure of less than 20 indicates an oversold situation, while a measure of greater than 80 indicates overbought.

Here's exactly how I use it:

In this chart, whenever the two lines of the stochastics enter into this overbought area (above the 80 level) or oversold area (below 20), it represents the possibility of some sort of a reversal back into the neutral area.

- For instance, if you are looking to establish a long position when the stochastics are in the overbought area, the probability of the trade working is diminished greatly.

- Conversely, if you are looking to establish a short position in the oversold area, that trade, too, has a lower probability of playing out.

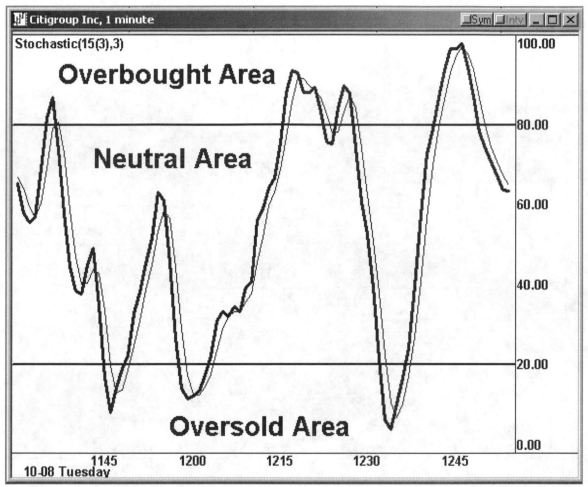

Figure 6-1

Before we go much further, let's define stochastics and the settings I use in my charts.

In terms of the setting I use for my charts (all time frames up to a daily chart), I use a 15,3,3 setting on a slow stochastic.

The image in Figure 6-2 shows how I plug those settings in, using Q-Charts. While the way you enter these settings will vary depending on your charting software, the important thing is that you are aware of exactly what the settings are.

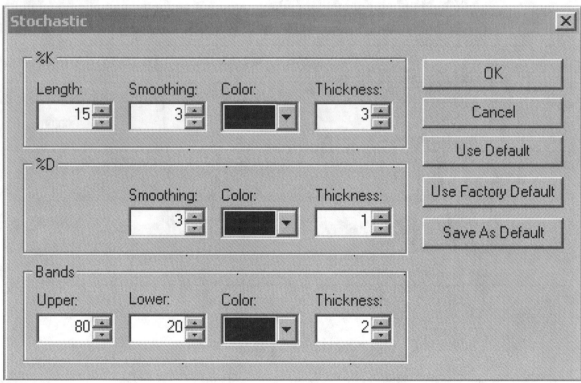

Figure 6-2

In using stochastics, we only want to concern ourselves with the following:

- Are the stochastics in an overbought/oversold condition?

- Is the thicker line (%K) on the verge of crossing above or below the thinner line (%D), which will indicate an imminent change in price direction?

Naturally, one question that will come to mind is:

If the stochastics are overbought, indicating some sort of a reversal, why don't you just get short?

This is the way in which stochastics is commonly misused. Let's see how.

Under MOST circumstances, in order for the stochastics to be in an overbought situation on a 1-minute chart, the trend would also need to be up. As discussed early on in this book, HVT is not a style which tries to buck the overall trend.

Referring back to this chart, if you had broken one of the cardinal rules of HVT (Trading With the Trend) and went short at X when the stochastics were overbought, would you have been rewarded? Absolutely not. In fact, the trade provided nothing but frustration.

Let's be generous and say that you sold the stock short at the high of that bar, $72.97. The lowest price, Point Y, was 72.89. It would have been very difficult if not impossible to have shorted and covered at those exact prices. If you were stubborn and did not try to cover at the low bar, the move at Point Z would have forced you out if you were adhering to money management rules.

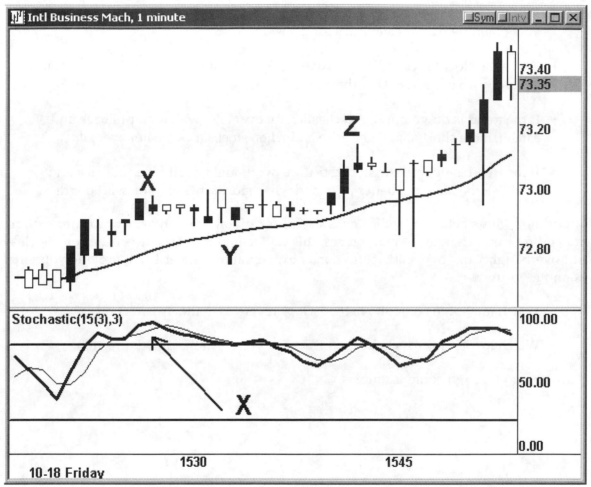

Figure 6-3

HOW TO KEEP YOUR FOCUS ON HIGH-PROBABILITY TRADES USING STOCHASTICS

To use stochastics to filter out high-risk trades so that you can only focus on the high-probability ones, use these simple rules of thumb:

- When the stochastics indicator is overbought, as signified by a reading above 80, you generally do not establish a long position

- When the stochastics indicator is oversold, as signified by a reading below 20, you generally do not establish a short position

- If the trend is down but the stochastics are oversold, wait for a pullback and establish the short at a better price and when stochastics are not oversold

- If the trend is up, but the stochastics are overbought, wait for a pullback and establish the long at a better price and when stochastics are not overbought

In addition, the stochastics indicator is useful for giving you an "early warning" of an impending trend change. In many cases, this can actually override the need for the classic "overbought" or "oversold" conditions I explain above. Later I will provide you with examples of this.

- Watch for %K to cross above the %D for reversals in the up direction

- Watch for %K to cross below the %D for reversals in the down direction

Now let's go through some examples.

Take at look at the chart in Figure 6-4. It is an hourly chart of IBM. Notice that the over-bought areas denoted by 1 and 2 indicate that if you entered a long position at that time, you decrease the probability of that trade working, by a large degree. The price action that follows shortly after is lower.

Figure 6-4

The chart in Figure 6-5 is also of IBM. This time the stock is in a downtrend, as noted by the moving average sloping downward. However, what is important in this chart is the stochastics. If you were looking to establish a short position in the area of 1 or 2, you will notice that the stochastics are in an oversold condition. These trades would have immediately gone against you.

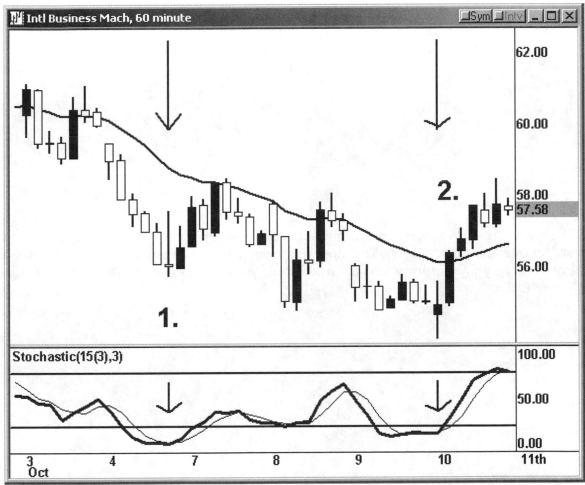

Figure 6-5

This is a chart of Wal-Mart on a 5-minute basis. Notice at the area denoted by 1, you have an overbought condition. This does not mean get short. If you did, the trade would have been very painful for you. That trade could have been avoided. The trend was up. Do not buck it.

Figure 6-6

ADVANCED STOCHASTICS STRATEGIES

For the rest of this chapter, I will be using 1-minute charts to illustrate some more advanced techniques and subtle approaches to using stochastics.

I will show you how to use stochastics as a filtering tool to alert you to setups as well as using them to help identify exits.

Don't worry if you don't quite grasp the nuances. I will be taking you through examples to help you get a feel for these concepts.

Look at the following examples of IBM and MSFT.

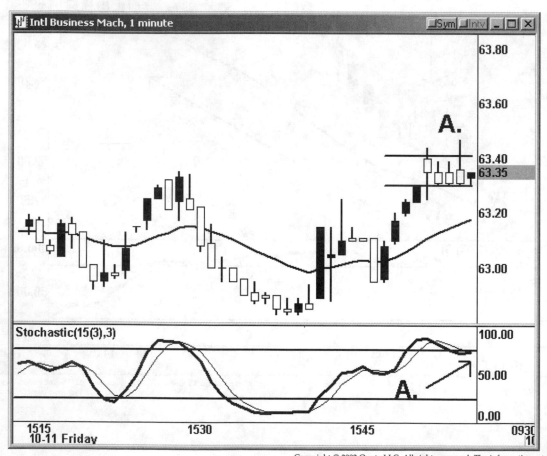

Figure 6-7

Figure 6-8

In these two charts, I see a potential long entry point at Point A. The first thing you might say is: "The stochastics are in an overbought situation."

Yes, they are *currently*. However, the trend is up and the stochastics have begun to *pull back and the price bars are consolidating*. This is the sign that a long trade is setting up. The trigger has not occurred yet, but I am now alerted to watch for it. Basically, when stochastics bends back up from its pullback and a confirmation is seen in the tick chart (see Chapter 8), then it may be time to go long.

I use stochastics as a filtering tool to alert me to setups as well as using them to help identify exits.

Here's what I look for:

1. A consolidation within a strong trend

2. Stochastics pulls back and then begins to curl back in the direction of the trend

3. The fast stochastic line begins to cross the slow stochastic line

These next charts simply reinforce the pattern we are trying to identify that offers the highest-probability setups. The stochastics are neither overbought nor oversold. They are simply exhibiting a pattern which shows the potential for a resumption of the trend (Point A).

The key thing to notice here is that I need to see the Fast Stochastic (thicker line) making an attempt at crossing the slow stochastic (thinner line) in order to consider an entry point. This is my heads up. Scanning your charts for consolidations in price, in and around the 20-period moving average in conjunction with the stochastics on the verge of turning, is how you spot the ideal setups.

As shown in these charts, a turn in the Stochastics might sometimes be accompanied by a pullback to the 20-period moving average. **While a pullback to the 20-period moving average is** *not a "buy signal" in itself*, **it does serve as a** *nice confirmation.*

Figure 6-9

In this example we have a down trend, with the price bars consolidating at the 20-period moving average. The stochastics, at Point A are beginning to indicate that further price erosion is possible.

Figure 6-10

A pull-back in an up-trend with the stochastics beginning to indicate a resumption of the trend, Point A.

Figure 6-11

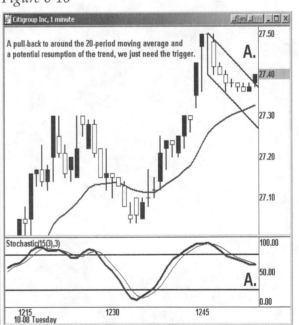

A pull-back to around the 20-period moving average and a potential resumption of the trend, we just need the trigger.

Figure 6-12

The 1-Minute Chart, Your GPS to Intraday Setups

> The victory goes to those who know how to patiently stalk high-probability trades . . .

While most people tend to focus on longer time frames for their trading ideas, and consider the 1-minute chart just a bunch of noise, the skillful trader will recognize that, regardless of the time frame you are trading on, the technical patterns that most traders use are clearly evident. That is true of the 1-minute chart. You will see just as many head-and-shoulder patterns, breakouts, reversals, etc., as you will on a daily chart. The difference is simply the duration of your trade. The other major difference is in how you determine exactly when to execute a trade. The answer lies in Chapter 8, where I teach you how to use tick charts. However, what is important at this point is that you will only be using the 1-minute chart.

I refer to the 1-minute chart as a Market GPS (Market Global Positioning Satellite). Why the clever name? Because it accurately describes the function of the 1-minute chart. Its only use, and I stress "only," is to help you identify POTENTIAL setups.

A 1-minute chart will show you where you are in relation to your surroundings, but in most cases offers you no advice or directions on how to get to your next destination. It simply shows you where you are. It is up to you to determine how to get to your destination. Under these circumstances you then refer to a local map or some other tool to assist you in finding your way.

So what will the 1-minute chart alert a trader to? First of all, and most importantly, you have to be able to identify the current trend as denoted by the slope of the 20-period moving average. Once that is established, we want to look at the chart and try to identify areas where the trend may have paused, but looks as though it is set to resume. The next two charts will illustrate the two setups which we always want to be on the lookout for: pullbacks in uptrends and rallies in downtrends. These two setups constitute 90% of the trades I do.

The Pullback in an Up-Trend

Notice that at each X Point there has not only been a pullback and consolidation of the price bars but the stochastics have also pulled back and are poised to confirm a resumption of the up-trend.

Important point: Typically when I am trading I am always referring to pullbacks <u>not in the price action but in the stochastics.</u>

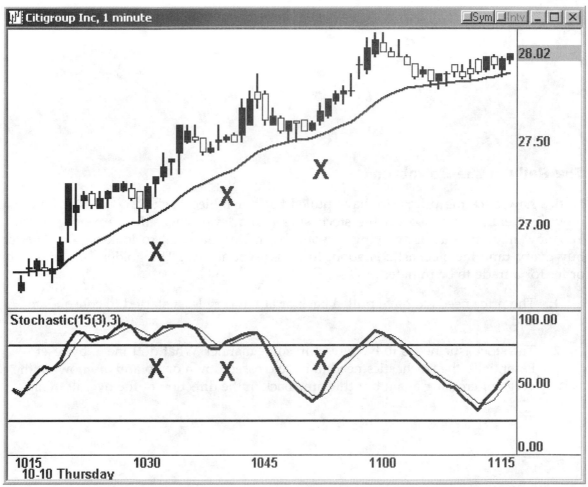

Figure 7-1

The Rally in the Downtrend

Notice how once the price bars have pulled back or rallied back towards the 20-period moving average, you also get the stochastics into a level where they are not oversold. You now have two items working in your favor. Do you want to look to sell short or buy every time the stochastic is about to cross? Not always. The golden rule is that in order for a trade to be initiated:

1. The price needs to have pulled back or at the very least started to consolidate and

2. The stochastic needs to have reset in some manner. What do I mean by reset? Essentially the stochastics need to have crossed down or up and are now on the verge of crossing again but this time back in the direction of the overall trend.

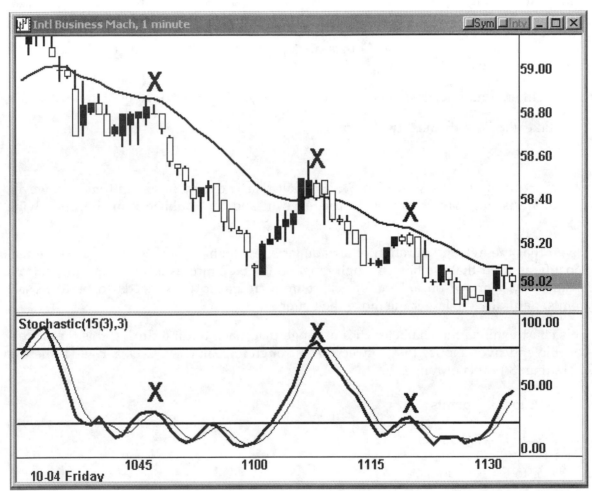

Figure 7-2

HOW 1-MINUTE BARS TELL YOU WHEN IT'S TIME TO STAY OUT OF THE MARKET

Another important aspect of analyzing the 1-minute bars is to make a determination as to whether or not there is enough range in the futures currently to even justify placing a trade. I have taught people over and over again about the importance of seeing a minimum of 3-point moves in the S&Ps and 5-10 points in the Nasdaq.

What do I mean by that? The futures are up or down that amount on the day? The range of the day thus far?

Neither. I am referring to what you have seen over the last 5, 10 or 15 minutes.

Take a look at the next two examples.

The chart in Figure 7-3 shows an S&P market that is clearly in an up-trend. However, that alone is not enough reason to try to go in and buy pullbacks in the underlying stocks.

Given that the average duration of a trade lasts less than 5 minutes, we need to be reasonably assured that we have enough range in the S&P futures in order to pull that off. Historically, a move on a 1-minute chart from trough to peak needs to be at least 3 points, naturally the larger the move the better.

This chart exhibits the characteristics of range that make trading during this time a reasonable endeavor. Notice that between each trough to peak (A-B, C-D, E-F, G-H) there is more than 3 points of range.

- A to B = 7 points

- C to D = 7.5 points

- E to F = 6.75 points

- G to H = 11 points

Certainly you cannot expect to be a buyer at the bottom and a seller at the top, as a practitioner of HVT you can only hope to grab the "meat" in between. But many times, that is a lot of meat.

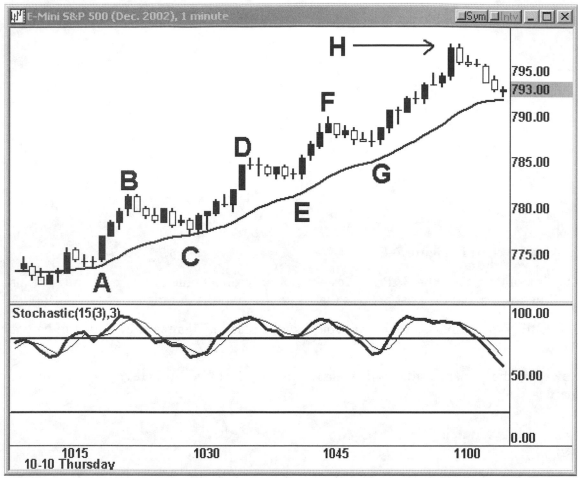

Figure 7-3

There are times when the market is not displaying 3 point+ ranges on the 1-minute chart. So how do you know when to start trading again?

1. Wait for a break of the current trading range

    OR

2. Wait for the S&Ps to start moving in 3 point+ bursts over the course of 5 to 10 minutes.

Look at the chart in Figure 7-4.

At this point in time the S&P futures are not only directionless, i.e., no trend, but also the little moves that do exist are less than 3 points in terms of range.

This is the type of market that you avoid like the plague. There is ZERO edge in here for HVT.

However, the patient trader will wait for this range to be broken as seen in the next chart.

Figure 7-4

The chart in Figure 7-5 is simply a continuation of the previous chart showing how the range is ultimately broken. Most traders will not have caught the move from A to B, but it does alert you to potential trading setups on the short side after a rally back to the 20-period moving average as seen on Points C and E.

So now that you are an expert at identifying setups on the 1-minute chart, let's focus on the next piece . . . entering and exiting trades at precisely the right moment.

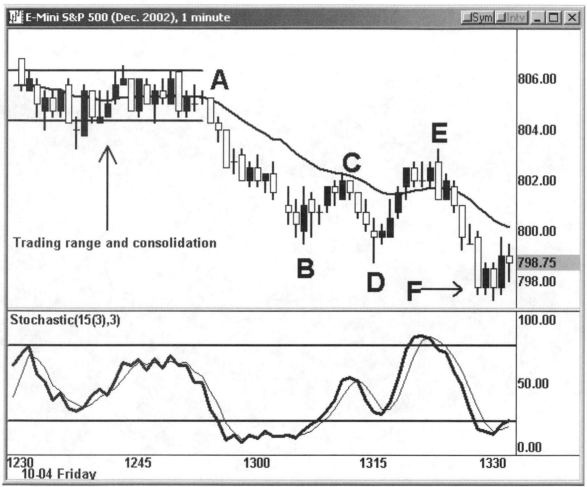

Figure 7-5

CHAPTER EIGHT

How to Use Tick Charts to Enter and Exit Trades

You've got the "ideal" setup in a powerful trend. Now here's the exact moment at which you pull the trigger . . .

Editor's note: the use of tick patterns is an important tool in David Floyd's trading strategy. However, historical tick data was not available for the examples in this book. In order to provide the best possible learning experience for the reader, Mr. Floyd hand-selected charts from his daily trading at the time this book was written. These charts, based upon his experience and expertise, replicate the tick patterns that would have accompanied specific trading examples in this book.

While most of you have already drawn the conclusion that this style of trading has a certain degree of "feel" built into it, nowhere is that more evident than in tick chart analysis.

A tick chart is simply a chart which shows EVERY change in price for a given security. I only use a tick chart of the S&P futures or the Nasdaq futures. It is not necessary to use on the individual stocks.

Why the importance? Simple. HVT, as you know by now, operates on the premise of small margins with tight stops. Just because we identify a potential setup on the 1-minute chart does not mean we rush right in and buy or go short. It is possible the trade may not develop for another minute or several minutes. Therefore, the anxious trader may need to endure being whipsawed until the trade plays out.

Let's look at this 1-minute chart in Figure 8-1. It shows the pullback of the S&P futures towards the 20-period moving average—a standard trade.

Like all trades, whether the setup is based on the daily chart, hourly or weekly chart, reversals rarely come in the form of an immediate turn. Rather, the trade develops over the course of several bars.

So, would you have been a buyer of the underlying stock using the futures as your guide at Point A or B?

Both answers are correct since ultimately the trade played out. However, which entry point(s) offered you immediate confirmation without the whipsaw action?

Answer: Point B.

But how do you know in advance that A is not the best entry point?

Point A is not confirmed by the stochastics. Price action is still moving lower.

Given the tight stops required, an entry at Point A may very well get stopped out and end up missing out on the big move once the trade does develop.

As an HVT Trader you need to wait for the exact moment that the market "bursts" in your direction. That is when you strike, when a rush of buyers or sellers is there to propel the futures and your stock in the direction you desire. It is this split-second response that separates the winners from the losers.

The tick chart simply allows you to put a microscope on the S&P or Nasdaq futures. You have already identified the setup on the 1-minute chart. Now the tick chart will allow you to strike at the most opportune time.

The formation we are looking for on a tick chart is simply one of consolidation followed by a breakout—similar to what you may see on a 1-minute chart.

Given that all charts, with the exception of tick charts, lag in terms of spotting the true setup, the tick chart is ABSOLUTELY REQUIRED. Yes, there is a degree of feel required. Simply establishing the position because the tick chart "breaks out" may not be valid.

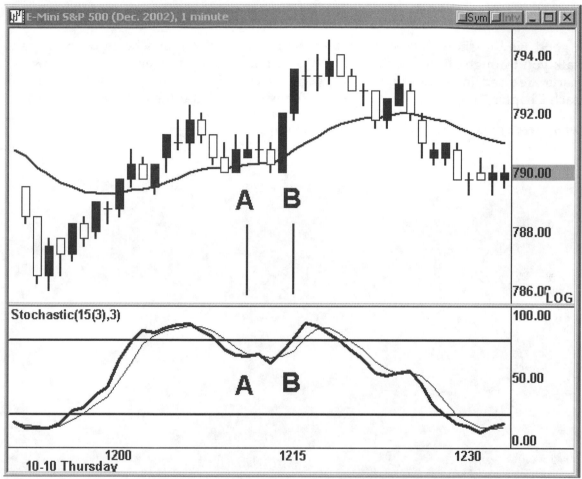

Figure 8-1

The move up or down in the tick chart needs to parallel the setup you are already stalking. If you were simply to trade every time the tick chart made an erratic move, you would go broke getting chopped up with price action and commissions.

PUTTING ALMOST ALL THE PIECES TOGETHER

A good way to show you where tick charts fit into the overall scheme of things is to walk you through all the trading tactics I've taught you *so far*. Then, you'll see how tick charts are used in conjunction with everything else. By the way . . . by the time you reach Chapter 14, you will be provided with my complete trading checklist.

Let's review what we have covered up until now:

Step 1: Determine the trend of the S&P futures on a 1-minute chart.

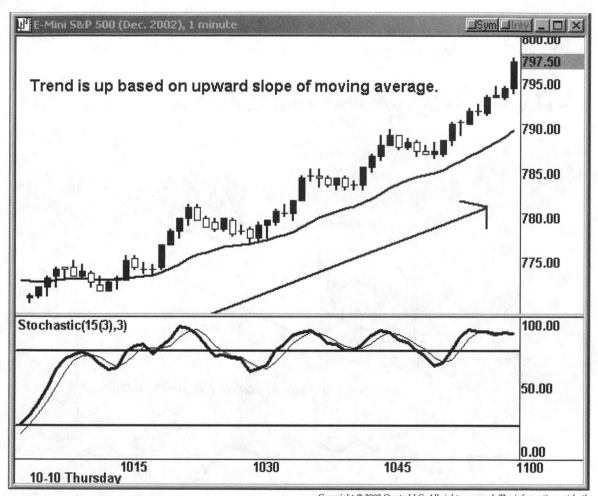

Figure 8-2

Step 2: Depending on the trend, look for a stock that is exhibiting a similar pattern and trading in tandem with the market.

If the trend is up, look for a stock that is trending up. The chart of Citigroup is clearly trending up. You will also notice that a stock like Citigroup (same industry group) will have almost an identical chart pattern to the 1-minute chart of S&P futures.

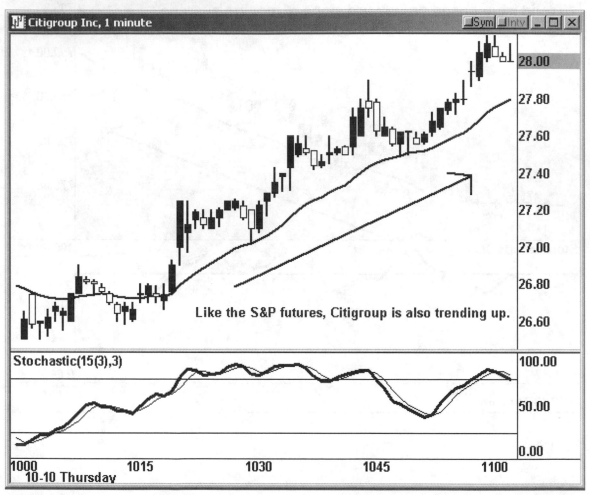

Figure 8-3

Step 3: On the 1-minute S&P chart, look for a pullback to begin forming.

Points A, B, and C all demonstrate areas where the price has pulled back indicating a potential resumption of the trend.

This is what the 1-minute chart is designed to do, to allow you to determine in a matter of seconds if there is an upcoming trade opportunity.

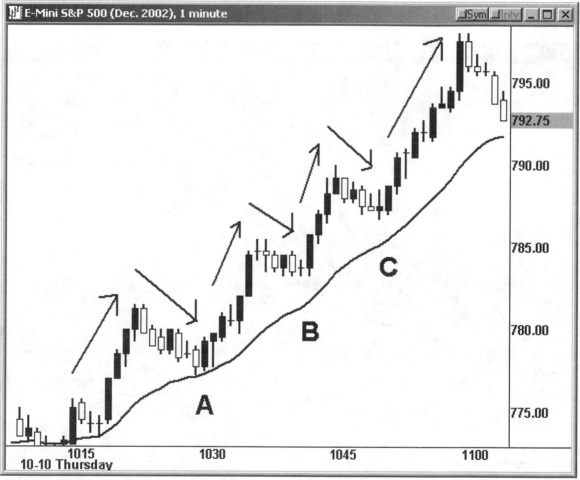

Figure 8-4

Step 4: Are the stochastics in an area where they, too, have pulled back? Remember, it does not always matter if the stochastics are in an overbought or oversold area. It just matters that they have pulled back and are looking to turn in the direction of the trend again. They do not necessarily need to go all the way back to oversold in order to justify the entry. Point A, B and C indicate this clearly. Notice how Point B, while still above the stochastic reading of 80, indicating an overbought area, still provides a great clue for a long entry point. The inverse of this is applicable for stocks that are in downtrends. If you are looking to get short, make sure that the stochastics have at least "rallied" a bit and are not pegged at oversold.

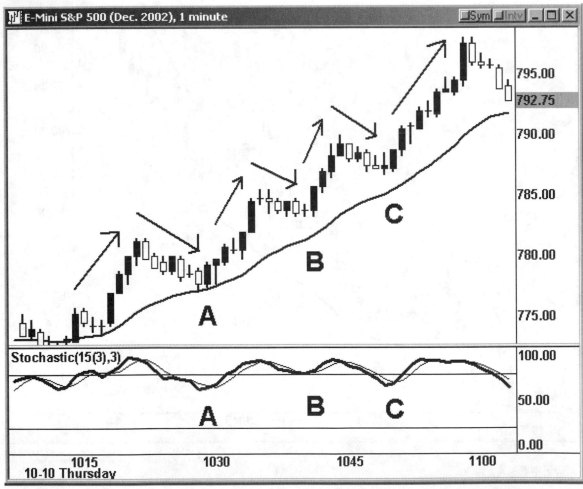

Figure 8-5

Step 5: Focus your attention now on the tick chart of the futures as well as the price action in the stock you anticipate playing in. Watch for a consolidation in the tick chart to burst in the direction of the setup you're stalking. That is when you enter the trade. You will learn how this is done when I walk you through real world examples. For now, I've provided you with the general concept and how it fits with the other pieces of my trading methodology.

Now let's describe the process of exiting a trade.

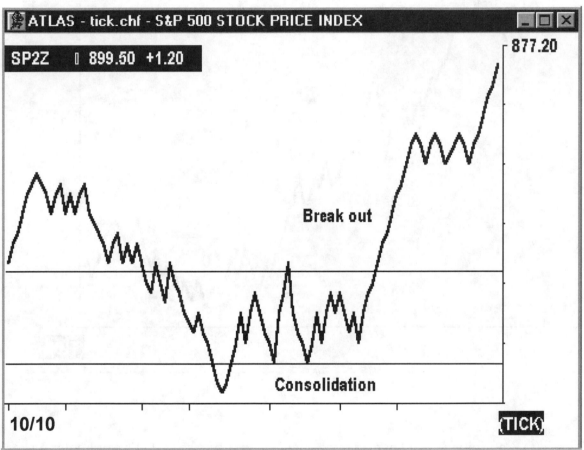

Figure 8-6

MY MAGICAL TOOL FOR EXITING TRADES

So what is the magical tool one can use to determine when to *exit* a trade? I refer back to the tick chart.

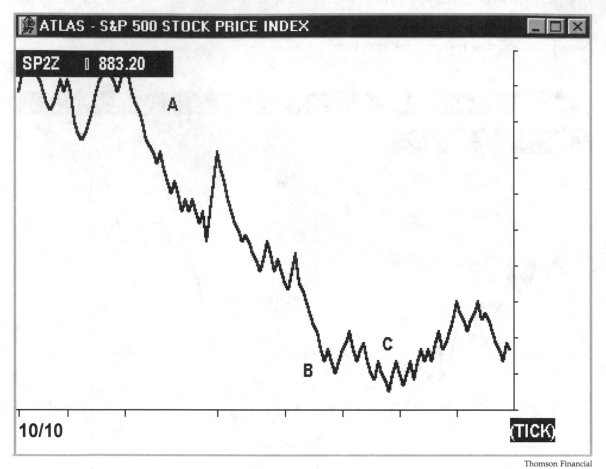

Figure 8-7

Notice that at Point A you have a strong downtrend assert itself. Let's say I enter a short position on that basis. The tick heads downward with little interruption until you get to the area between Point B and Point C when the downward momentum in the S&Ps begins to lose ground. At the time this is happening, you don't know whether it is a short pause or perhaps the end of the move down. Since there is absolutely no way to tell, I will exit the position in its entirety, using a MARKET ORDER. That's my entire exit technique. When I see trend momentum weakening in the tick chart, I get out of the trade.

Now you might be asking, why a market order? Simple. At this point I just want out of the trade. It is obvious from the tick chart that buyers have come in and the price is beginning to deteriorate. That doesn't mean that the price won't continue to go in the direction of the trade I've exited. But I'm not taking any chances. If I try to get cute and pick a price, and miss getting filled, by the time I cancel and re-enter the order I would have probably received a better fill by simply giving a market order originally.

Yes, there will be times when a limit order would have worked better, but more times than not the market order will get you the better exit price.

There are times when I will choose to exit only half of my position. These times are infrequent, but they are signified by large spikes up or down in the futures, typically driven by news events or the like. Sometimes the strategy works well. Sometimes you would have been better off exiting the whole position at once.

If this sounds too insanely simple, I can only tell you that it has worked for me and those I have personally trained, for several years. You have to keep in mind that in HVT, we are in the market for quick profits. We want to take money off the table at the first sign of weakness in the 1-minute trend because our chances of locking in a winning trade at that point are the very greatest.

The added benefit of using the tick chart to exit is that when there is a losing trade, it is shut down very quickly and the losses are kept to a minimum. Even though I use a mental stop that is based on price, watching for weakening momentum on a tick chart always gets me out before that price stop is hit.

In essence, you could say that "weakening momentum" is the stop-loss that HVT traders use.

CHAPTER NINE

Gaining "Big-Picture" Awareness with 5-Minute Charts

Is there a way for us to know how rewarding the NEXT setup will be? Yes, here's how . . .

Up to this point we have focused exclusively on 1-minute and tick charts. However, no HVT approach would be complete without a 5-minute chart. The 5-minute chart is not a timing indicator! Rather, I use it in a similar fashion to the way I use stochastics, as a screening mechanism. Let's say we have been trading IBM actively for the last 40 minutes or so, buying the pullbacks in the uptrend.

Is there a way for us to know when the NEXT setup will not be as rewarding as the previous ones? Or more importantly not even worth taking based on the risk/reward analysis?

Yes, the 5-minute chart. Let's get right to some examples.

Stepping back a moment, let's look at our previous entry points on IBM, as denoted by Point X. The big question now is:

Will Point Y in the next few minutes also provide another pullback entry on the long side?

Point Y is starting to show signs as a valid re-entry point on the long side.

- The price has pulled back to the 20-period moving average.

- The stochastics have pulled back and may begin to turn back up.

So at this point it is a matter of waiting to see if the trade develops. From what you have learned up to this point, I would not argue. However, the 5-minute chart of IBM tells us a different story and also lets us know there is no need to wait around to see if the trade does develop, it likely will not.

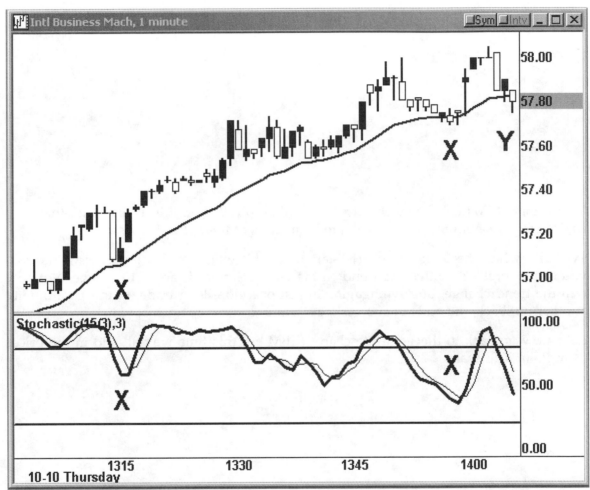

Figure 9-1

Notice that at Point Y, the stochastics are starting to roll-over. It is at this point that long trades off the 1-minute chart start to erode in terms of their effectiveness.

Typically when the 5-minute charts start to exhibit what I call "stochastic weakness," you can be pretty sure that the trend on the 1-minute chart is about to change. Not only will the trend change, but by engaging in just one more long trade, in this case buying another pullback, the odds of success are starting to stack up against you.

Let's now go back to the 1-minute chart of IBM but this time we will add in the prices from Point Y forward.

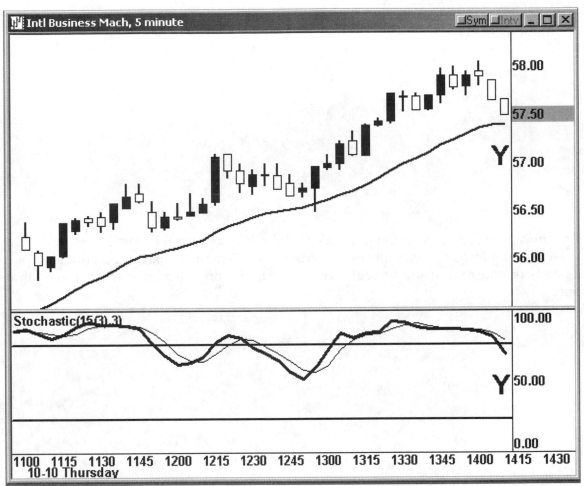

Figure 9-2

As you can see, an entry to the long side at Point Y would have been a losing trade. This illustrates the importance of always referring to the 5-minute chart, especially after periods where you have made several consecutive trades off a 1-minute chart in one direction.

Figure 9-3

The HVT Screen Layout

Here's how to keep a clear, focused view of the trading battlefield . . .

OK, now I have covered all my basic patterns and indicators. While I do have some special techniques which we've yet to cover, it's time to start shifting gears from learning the tools to putting them all together and applying them. We still have a ways to go before walking through actual trading examples. But with this chapter we are beginning to make the transition to more of application emphasis.

Given the nature of my trading style, it is necessary to now look at how your screens should be set up so that you can integrate the 1-minute and tick charts into your visual space to achieve maximum efficiency. While the screen shot is of three screens, you can achieve the same results with two screens. Unfortunately, a one-screen layout is not functional.

The key, in my opinion, is to have everything laid out in a manner that allows you to shift from one section of your layout to the other, in a way that is sequential with the whole thought process, before entering a trade.

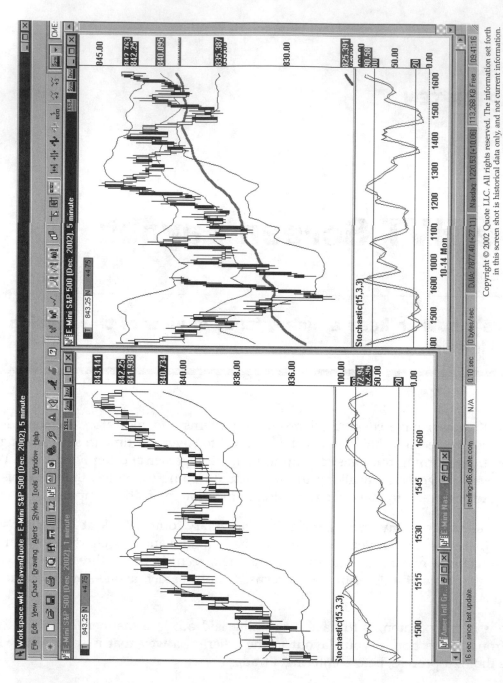

Figure 10-1 The Right Monitor

The right monitor contains what I consider the two most important charts on my layout, a 1- and 5-minute chart of the S&P 500 futures. It is here where I decide what setup I will be looking for. Will I be looking to get long, or will I be looking to get short?

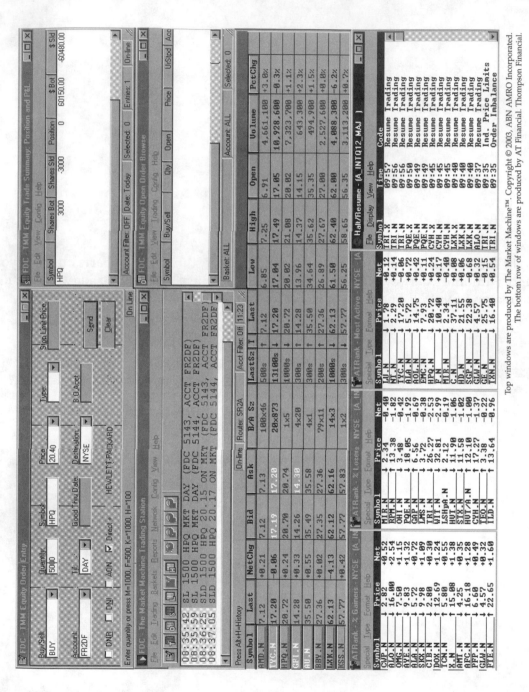

Figure 10-2   The Center Monitor

Top windows are produced by The Market Machine™. Copyright © 2003, ABN AMRO Incorporated. The bottom row of windows are produced by AT Financial. Thompson Financial.

The center monitor is where I spend the majority of my time once I have determined that I would like to establish a trade. This is the monitor where I keep a tick chart of the S&Ps, order entry boxes, and a comprehensive quote sheet.

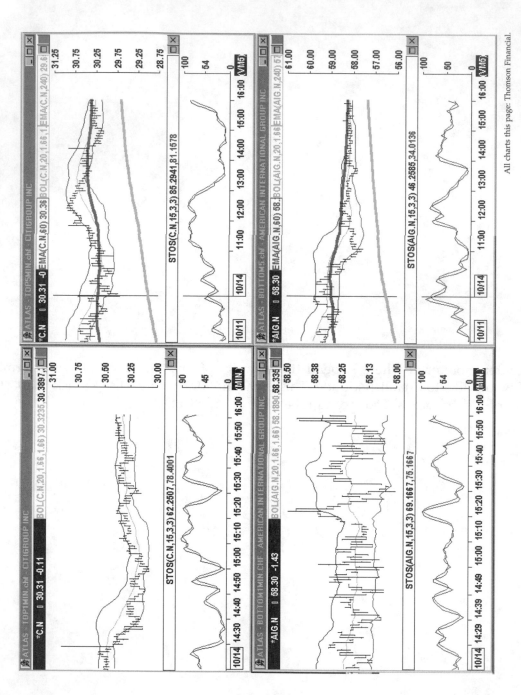

Figure 10-3 The Left Monitor

The left monitor is where I can look at the stocks that I may be trading on any given day. I have two stocks, each on two different time frames, 1- and 5-minute. Ideally what I am looking for is the 1-minute chart on either of these stocks to mirror the technical pattern of the 1-minute chart of the S&Ps. When I see this, I know there is a potential setup.

CHAPTER ELEVEN

How to Use the Level I Quote Screen and Place Orders

Huh . . . is that a typo? Surely, I must mean Level II. Nope. Let me explain why . . .

I am going to make the assumption that you are aware that in order to even have a chance of competing effectively at HVT, you need a Direct Access Broker. This type of trading CANNOT be accomplished via a discount broker.

Early on in this book, Chapter 3 to be exact, I spoke of the need to limit the information you get fed down to only those things which help you make money in the markets. Well, that not only applies to limiting the number of stocks you trade but also the amount of quote information you get. So again, flying in the face of convention, I am an advocate of the basic Level I Quote Screen which gives you:

Bid Ask Quote Size Last trade Volume High Low

Most if not all traders are more accustomed to using a Level II to monitor the stocks they are trading. With the exception of not being able to see the "depth" of the market on a Level I, there really are not that many differences.

My feeling is that seeing the so-called "depth" through Level II of the market is just pure illusion anyway. What knowledgeable trader or market maker is going to reveal their hand for the whole world to see? If anything, most large bids and offers are probably there more as a way of testing the market or as a device to fish for stock.

For example, let's say a floor broker needs to work a large order for a client, say 200,000 shares, with a specified price range for the fills. The floor broker cannot simply walk up to the specialist and expect to get the order done all at once, although that is possible. Instead, the floor broker will need to work that order. He may do that in a number of different ways. He may put up a big offer in the middle of a little sell-off in the futures as a way of "coaxing" in some sellers. At this point the floor broker may say to the specialist, "I'll take 25,000 of whatever comes in down to 67.25." Once he is filled, he may pull the offer. Naturally this does not come without risk to the floor broker. A large buyer may see that offer posted by the floor broker and take it. However, floor brokers, like all professionals, know how to navigate with minimal risk.

Obviously, the same practice can be done on the Nasdaq by way of ECNs. Instinet may have a large offer, but Merrill Lynch is on the bid buying everything that comes in.

You get the point. There is never any foolproof way to determine what is going on. However, over time you will notice certain nuances, especially if you trade the same stocks every day. Remember that you are interacting with other human beings, and human beings are famous for repeating patterns over and over again.

There is not a set of rules which I can give you to teach you all of these things. Simply stated, many times they contradict one another and it ends up leading to more confusion than clarification. The only way you will pick up on this is through constant observation.

That being said, more times than not, your basis for the trade will be based on the technical setup anyway. Reading the tape simply offers you a sharper edge. You do not need to become an expert tape reader in order to employ HVT. However, I believe it will make a big difference to your bottom line.

HOW TO PLACE ORDERS AND GET THEM EXECUTED THE HVT WAY

As I mentioned earlier, I am not trying to be Mr. Cute by buying on the bid so that I can capture that extra nickel on a trade, yet risk losing 10-15 cents because I was wrong. I keep it real simple. If the stock is going up, I am trying to buy the offer. If the stock is going down, I simply hit the bid.

My number one rule however is to always enter a trade with a Limit order, but always exit a trade with a Market order. The rationale is quite simple:

If the buying opportunity I have spotted is indeed valid and there happens to be a lot of competition from other traders trying to execute the same trade, you can bet that when the specialist gets "hit" with all these buy orders, he is going to take action. If he has plenty of stock on his book for sale at higher levels, he will do nothing, the matching process will simply take over. However, if there is little to no stock on the book, he is the one that needs to take the opposite side of the trade. And guess what? It won't be at the current offer price, it will more than likely be quite a bit higher. Hence, the need for limit orders. Now what I will do many times is place limit orders above the offer price to go long, or if I am going short place limit sell orders below the current bid.

Why would I do that?

Simple. If the move appears to be serious in terms of its potential, I WANT TO BE ON BOARD. I am willing to pay up, but not give a market order.

For instance, if the current market in IBM is as follows:

104.30 × 104.40 with a bid size of 25 and an offer size of 15, I may put in a limit order of Buy 2,000 IBM @ 104.50.

My thought process: It appears as though the S&Ps are about to make a big move above recent resistance. IBM, being a volatile stock with great intraday range, has the potential to move up 20–30 cents. Do I want to take the chance of trying to buy that 104.40 offer with only 1,500 shares on it and potentially miss it, or do I want to take out a little insurance policy and pay up 10 cents and have a better chance of getting filled? The answer to me is obvious.

One thing to remember though, just because you place the order above the current offer or below the current bid, does not mean that you will get that price. You may very well be the first order to hit the book and be filled at 104.40.

Obviously this type of strategy also requires a fair degree of subjectivity. You do not want to be paying up or down if there is very little volatility and the prospect for a large move is slim. It is a dynamic process and one that needs to be evaluated on a trade by trade basis.

CHAPTER TWELVE

How to Short Stocks Without Being Subject to the "Uptick Rule"

They keep talking about how they are going to get rid of the "uptick rule" and we all keep waiting. Here's what you can do in the meantime . . .

Have you ever been frustrated by trying to get short and not getting a good fill simply because you had to wait for the uptick? That problem is now solved. While bullets (married puts) and conversions have been around for some time, they are now routinely used by professional daytraders in order to play the short side of the market without getting whacked by the uptick rule.

So what are bullets?

Bullets, or married puts, are nothing more than long a deep in-the-money put and long stock. This is an APPROXIMATELY neutral position. In other words, regardless of what the market does, the value of the bullet position remains flat.

Here's what gives you the ability to short without being subject to the uptick rule:

You own the stock. Therefore, you can sell it.

Now here's where it gets a little abstract and just about everybody I explain this to gets a little glassy eyed. So I'll try to explain it as best I can.

Brokerage firms which sell the bullet product, sell it as a package. It is held in an account that is separate from your trading account. The fact that you own the stock in that account gives you the right to sell it in your trading account. Selling it in your account is the same thing as shorting it, because you will be buying it back, hopefully at a lower price. But you are not subject to the uptick rule because you own the stock.

The beauty of this comes from the fact that while you have a long position in the stock, it is 100% hedged by the long put option.

This gets around the uptick rule since you can sell the stock, uptick or no uptick, since you own it! Equally important, while you hold the bullet intact (long put/long stock), you don't make or lose money, so in effect you have "cocked the trigger" and are ready to "short." Bullets are usually used for one-day events, like news stocks, etc.

Frankly the technical structure of a bullet is not nearly as important as understanding the effectiveness of a bullet. As described above, when a negative news event hits the market do you really think you will be able to get a short off by waiting for an uptick? Forget about it. You need to be able to do what futures traders and traders of ETFS (Exchange Traded Funds) do, simply sell the security.

Keep in mind that this is not intended as a detailed "how to" on bullets. Rather, I just want to expose you to the concept. You can get more information about the actual mechanics from your broker.

CHAPTER THIRTEEN

How to Win the War Before the Battle Begins

> **Before the market even opens, you should have a good idea of where the best setups will be. Here's how . . .**

The following chapter is for advanced traders only and is optional. In it, I will teach you how to gain an added edge in pinpointing entries and exits using the Floyd Numbers. To use these techniques requires that you already have knowledge of Fibonacci and a wide range of support and resistance strategies. While the Floyd Numbers can enable you to be more selective with your trades, they are not a prerequisite for you to become a successful HVT trader.

At this point I have got you to the basic understanding of how trade setups are identified. However, many, if not all of the great setups come off of technical levels. So, if you can identify a standard setup, buying a pullback or selling short a rally that coincides with a critical technical level, you will have better probability of having a winning trade. Knowing some very basic things to look for, and more importantly how to integrate them in to your trading regimen will enhance your performance.

I start off each day by looking at the S&P and Nasdaq futures on multiple time frames, as well as the underlying stocks which I will be trading.

Time frames which I look at and consider to be the most critical:

- Weekly

- Daily

- Hourly

- 5-minute

Naturally this progression to shorter and shorter time frames serves to pinpoint if there is any confluence of levels on more than one time frame.

While looking at these charts, I am looking mainly for:

- 50- and 200-day exponential moving averages

- Fibonacci retracements and extensions

- Gap prices

- Previous lows and highs

- Break-ups or break-downs of trend lines/regression channels.

Let's walk through a scenario which happened at a critical time during the 2002 market. It was a re-test of the July lows of 771.

Figure 13-1—Naturally, the first thing I notice by looking at the daily chart is that the price action is approaching the lows. This in itself will be significant.

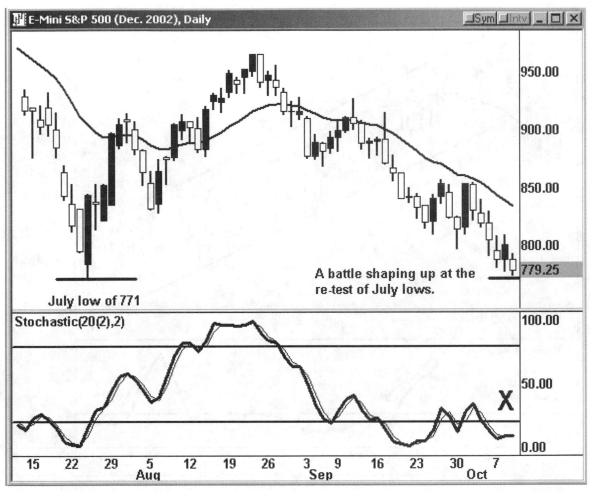

Figure 13-1

Figure 13-2—Now with all this setting up potentially on the daily chart, I looked at the hourly chart. The downward trend we had been in since Oct. 2 was getting pretty oversold, as noted by the stochastic reading of almost zero.

Figure 13-2

Figure 13-3—Looking at stocks that I trade on a day-to-day basis is also very helpful, in this case, a daily chart of Citigroup.

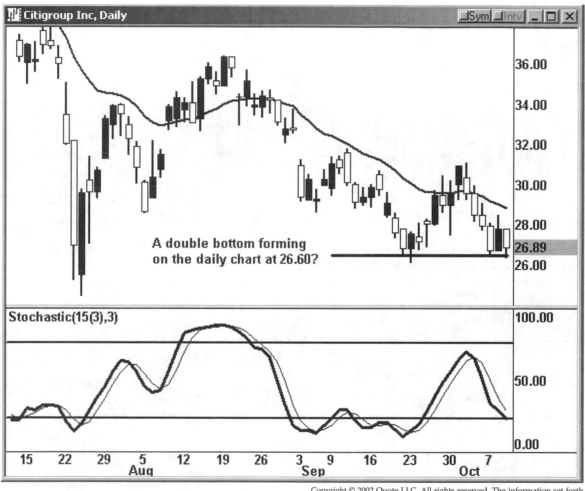

Figure 13-3

Figure 13-4—In this case we can see that the 26.60 level has been very key in recent sessions. Even though this level appears on the daily chart, it will still offer opportunities for HVT as well . . .

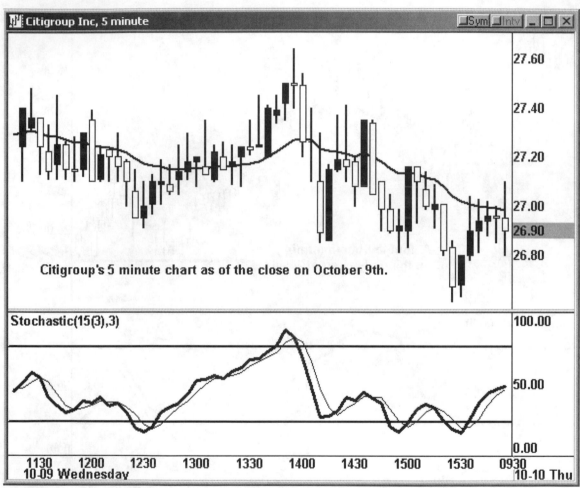

Figure 13-4

Figure 13-5—As a result, I will draw this line in on my 5-minute chart of Citibank. By drawing the line into the next day's data field it will provide you a clear vantage point when the price data is filled in.

Will this level be significant? Let's see . . .

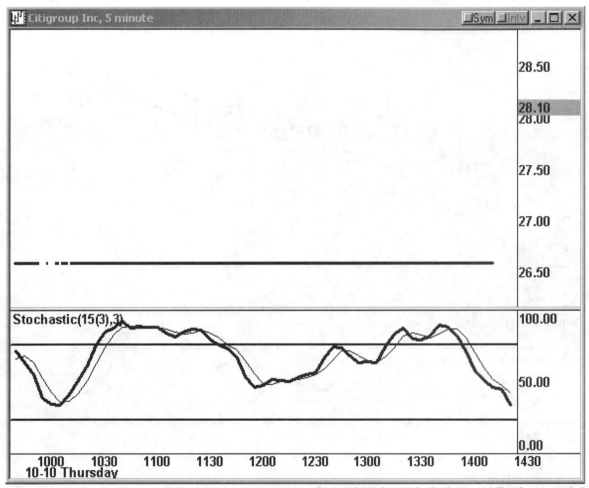

Figure 13-5 Daily chart support drawn in pre-market.

By looking at Point X, it becomes obvious that not only is the level significant on a daily chart, but significant on a 5-minute time frame as well. Additionally, the stochastics are oversold and on the verge of crossing at the same time. These are two very significant reasons for a bounce.

Fibonacci levels are also very important.

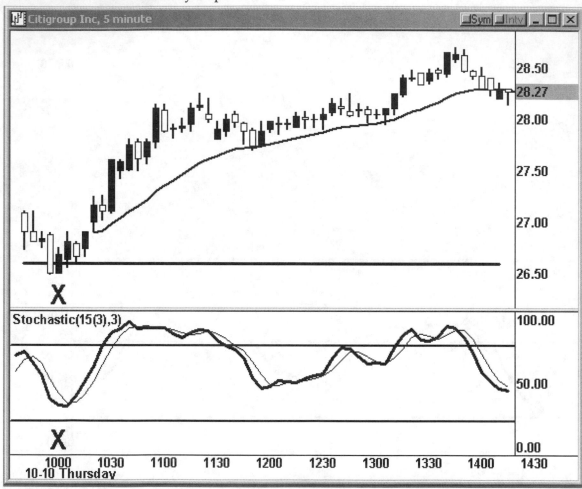

Figure 13-6

Again, like the above chart, when these levels are approached the following day, it offered a very nice reference point for a potential resumption of the up-trend.

Figure 13-7—Notice at Point X, the S&P futures are touching the 37.5% retracement off of the previous day's low. This level also coincides with an oversold stochastic which offers further evidence of a trend change in the short-term.

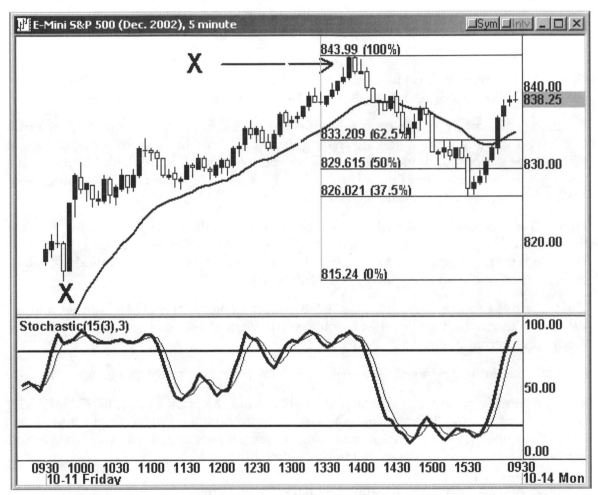

Figure 13-7

So I have established that there is an edge in knowing about price levels at which there are multiple reasons for the price action to be deflected in one direction or another. I will now explain how I compile these levels after the market closes and then put them to use in the next day's trading.

After the market closes each day, I identify all the key support and resistance levels for the S&P Futures and 3 or 4 stocks that I am trading. I pay particular attention to situations in which there are an especially high number of support or resistance factors all stacking up simultaneously.

Next, I go to my 1- and 5-minute charts and draw horizontal lines at these "super" support or resistance levels and extend them into the next day.

For instance, let's say I have been trading American International Group (AIG) recently and intend to trade it the following trading day. I will draw in the lines for all the levels that may be support and resistance. If I show you this chart, it won't look like much. It's just a set of horizontal lines on a blank white background. But each of these lines is of great significance in my trading.

They allow me to anticipate where the best potential trading setups are going to form the next day. In HVT, you have to decide very quickly whether you're going to commit your money. Having the Floyd Numbers at my disposal through the trading day enables me to make these decisions quickly and confidently.

The thing to keep in mind is that the levels simply depict POTENTIAL support and resistance numbers for the day ahead. You don't trade off these alone. In this case it is for American International Group (AIG).

Now let's see how significant these levels were the following trading day.

The first thing you notice is that two of the FNs from the night before, 57.97 and 59.40, were very significant. The key thing here is to notice how they played right into an existing "buy the pull-back" setup. Knowing these numbers coincided with that should give you far more conviction on the trade playing out.

- Point X: a price pullback and potential stochastic cross

- Point Y: a stochastic cross

This was a trade where I increase my share size to take advantage of the higher-probability outcome.

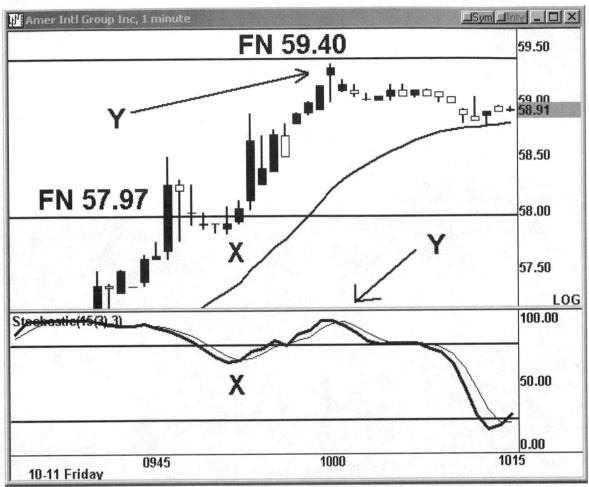

Figure 13-8

Once you have determined the critical technical levels for the day ahead, it is imperative that you draw them onto the 1 and 5-minute chart of that security. By doing this they will be in your line of sight throughout the trading day and you can see where the best trading opportunities are most likely to form.

CHAPTER FOURTEEN

Your Daily HVT Trading Checklist

Here is how you use all that I have taught you to daytrade successfully . . .

In this section, you will learn how to apply all the trading knowledge that I have taught you to the real world. I will take you through the bread-and-butter trading setups that I apply each and every day . . . plus some more advanced ones. **But you should know that I do not make an effort to get fancy. Ninety percent of what I trade are pullbacks from stocks in strong uptrends and rallies in strong downtrends.**

To execute these trades, I have an "assembly line" mentality. I just go down the same checklist every time. Once you can go down that same checklist, you will know how I earn my paycheck.

On the following page, I will show you my checklist. From there, I will show you example after example of how I apply it to actual trades I have done.

The HVT Checklist:

☑ Determine the trend in the S&P Futures on a 1-minute chart.

☑ Look for the same trend in the individual stock that you are looking to trade on a 1-minute chart.

☑ Identify pullbacks within the *trend in stochastics* in both the S&P futures and the stock.

☑ Identify pullbacks within the *price trend* in both S&P futures and the stock.

☑ Identify that a resumption of trend in S&P futures and stochastics is beginning.

☑ Enter limit order in stock on "market burst pattern" in S&P Futures tick charts.

☑ Watch for the momentum to slow down in stochastics and the tick chart.

☑ Exit at market on first sign of weakening of the trend as indicated by the tick chart.

Actual stop-loss orders are impractical, given the fast pace of HVT. While you should use mental stops, I do not include it in this checklist because when you are using your tick charts properly, your mental stop should never get hit, whether or not the trade goes in your favor.

BUYING PULLBACKS—EXAMPLE 1

Now, in this and the following examples, I will show you exactly how to apply this simple checklist to your trading. Referring to Figures 14-1 and 14-2 . . .

☑ Are the S&P futures in an uptrend on the 1-minute chart?

☑ If yes , is the 1-minute chart of the stock you are trading also in an uptrend, and more importantly, exhibiting a similar pattern as the futures?

☑ Are the stochastics pulling back and not in an overbought condition?

If you answered yes to these questions, then you have a scenario that will look like this:

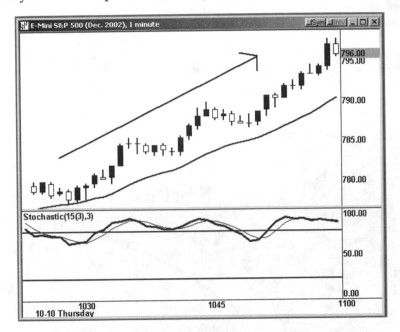

Figure 14-1

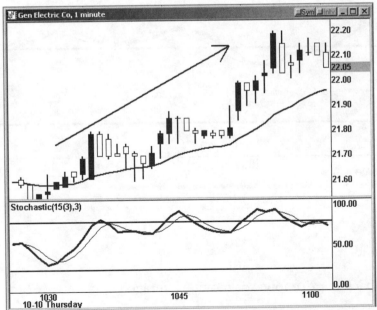

Figure 14-2

☑ Next, you must ask yourself: **Are the futures pulling back towards the moving average, consolidating and on the verge of moving back up?** If so, the S&Ps will look like this.

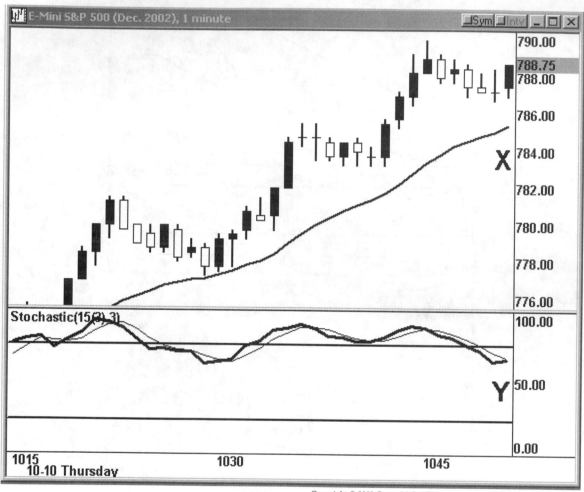

Figure 14-3

Look at both X and Y:

- X: A pullback in price towards moving average

- Y: A potential re-cross of the stochastics

And also notice the GE 1-minute chart, it looks almost identical:

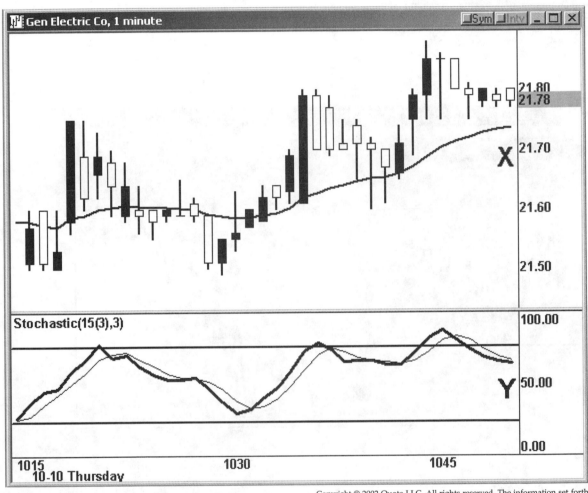

Figure 14-4

Again we have the same setup as described above. Look at both X and Y:

- X: A pullback in price towards moving average

- Y: A potential recross of the stochastics

☑ Now, referring to Figure 14-5, we are simply waiting for the S&P futures to make a quick spike to the upside, this will indicate a resumption of the trend.

The move back above the horizontal line is the trigger that you are looking for. The tick chart displays perfectly the pullback in the futures, a brief consolidation, before a quick upward "burst" which resumes the trend.

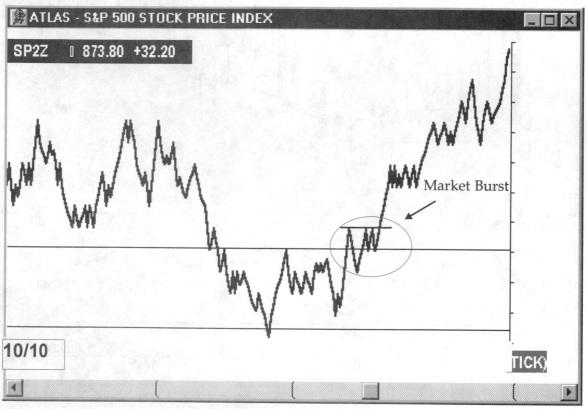

Figure 14-5

While the tick chart was setting up, I was also keeping a close eye on the market in GE so that I would know exactly what price to enter to establish a long, if and when the trigger was activated.

Bid	Ask	Bid/Ask Size	Last	Last Size
21.76	21.80	10 × 44	21.78	500

Most traders will approach this market with the following thought:

If the S&Ps make a move up, I will enter an order to buy 1,000 shares at 21.80.

> While I would not argue with the logic, keep in mind that there are only 4,400 shares on the offer. **Are you going to be quick enough to get there before someone else takes those shares?** That is not a bet I am willing to take.

My rule of thumb is this:

If there is less than 5,000 shares on the offer (or bid for short sales), pay up. Wouldn't you rather pay up and get the trade than try to be stingy and miss out on the move? Paying up is an insurance policy without the drawbacks of placing a market order.

Keep in mind that unlike the Nasdaq, just because you place a limit order above the offer price, it does not mean you will get only that price. Everything on the NYSE is based on time stamps. If you get there first, you get whatever is available.

> ☑ So, I would enter an order to buy 2,000 shares at 21.85.

I got filled at 21.80.

> ☑ And I watch for the momentum to slow down in stochastics and the tick chart.

The futures make a run of 8 points, from 789 (Point X) to 797 (Point Y) before losing momentum. Also at this time the stochastics began to cross back down (Point Z).

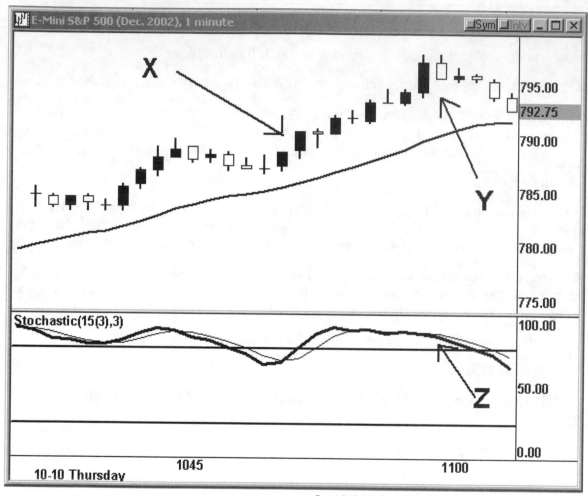

Figure 14-6

This can also be seen in the tick chart as well.

Notice that there are two notations that I have drawn in on this chart, each represents an area where the S&Ps appear to be losing their upward momentum. Typically, I will exit a position when I begin to see this, or at the very least get rid of half. This is an insurance policy in the event the market regains the momentum, as it did in this case.

The next time the momentum begins to slow down is when you call it quits on the trade. Ninety-nine percent of the time, the moves that HVT traders play off are short in duration. This one was about 4–5 minutes. By staying in any longer, you significantly increase the probabilities of giving back your gains on the trade.

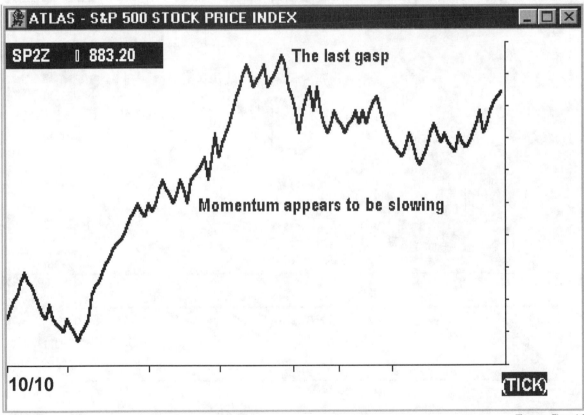

Thomson Financial

Figure 14-7

The 1-minute chart of GE accurately reflects the price action in the S&P futures.

Point X was the breakout from consolidation and resumption of upward trend, Point Y was the "last gasp" for the meat of the move, and Point Z confirms that with a stochastic cross. As this played out, my quote of GE looked like this:

Bid	Ask	Bid/Ask Size	Last	Last Size
22.10	22.20	100 × 30	22.18	500

☑ Time to exit. I sent in a market order to sell 2,000 shares, I was filled at 22.12, a 32 cent gain.

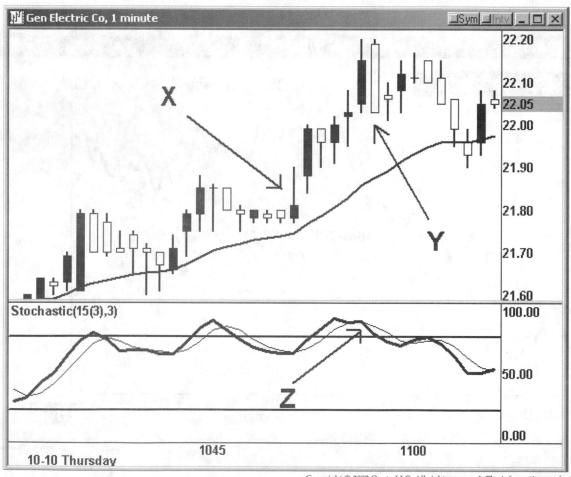

Figure 14-8

CHAPTER 14

BUYING PULLBACKS—EXAMPLE 2

Frankly, my job as a HVT trader resembles one of a guy on the assembly line. I do the same thing over and over again. The preceding trade I walked you through is no different from many thousands of other trades I have made.

I know that does not sound very glamourous, but I want to emphasize that I am in this business *for the money and not the excitement.*

So the expectation that I will go into work each day having a set routine with little deviation from it, is my edge. I meet traders all the time who have a different attitude. They expect the market to throw them curve balls and they gear themselves up to react strategically and creatively to them. I do not believe that I am smart enough to be able to do this every day. I would question whether anybody is. Dealing with unknown variables exposes me to risk that is not conducive to making a steady living and supporting my family through my trading business. I shun the unknown and embrace only those situations that I am intimately familiar with.

And I keep it very simple. All the rest of my trading examples demonstrate this. Since I trade the same two to four stocks every day—and I usually go after the same kind of setup, either pullbacks in uptrending markets or rallies in downtrending markets— you'd expect that many of the trades would look the same.

Here is another example of a trade that is setting up as a viable long position.

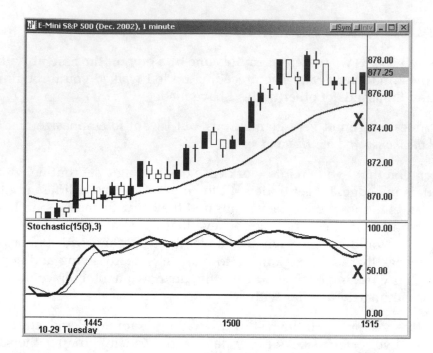

Figure 14-9

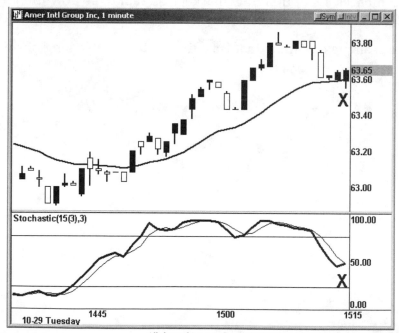

Figure 14-10

Let's start going down the list.

☑ What's the trend in the S&Ps and the stock I'm watching? Both the S&P futures and AIG are in an uptrend as noted by their upwardly sloping moving averages.

☑ Are stochastics pulling back? The price as well as the stochastics have pulled back and have begun to consolidate (Points X).

☑ As is always the case, you need the trigger which is the tick chart. We're watching for it to start moving . . . and it does (Point A).

Thomson Financial

Figure 14-11

At the time, the market on AIG was as follows:

Bid	Ask	Bid/Ask Size	Last	Last Size
63.60	63.65	10 × 25	63.62	500

My rule of thumb is simple, if there is less than 5,000 shares on the offer I will pay up.

☑ I entered an order as such:

Buy 1,000 AIG at 63.70

My fill was at 63.70.

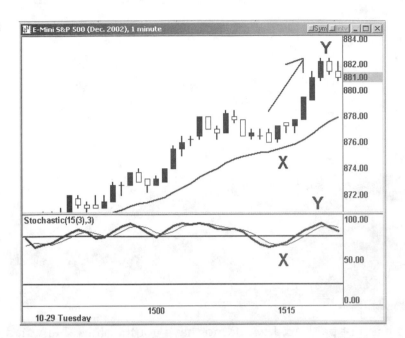

Figure 14-12

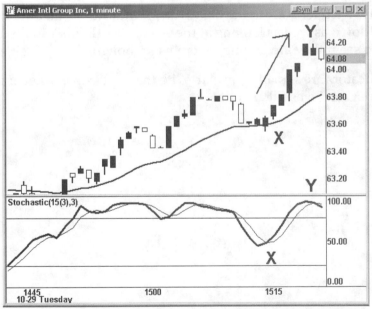

Figure 14-13

In this case if I had not paid up, I would not have got the stock. I am glad that I did, by paying up a nickel, I was able to capture the following move:

☑ Naturally, we refer back to the tick chart for indications that the momentum is slowing down as well as looking at the stochastics (Point Y in the previous two charts) to see if they are getting severely overbought.

☑ Both indicators are signaling an exit. With that, I place a market order: Sell 1,000 AIG at market. I was filled at 64.

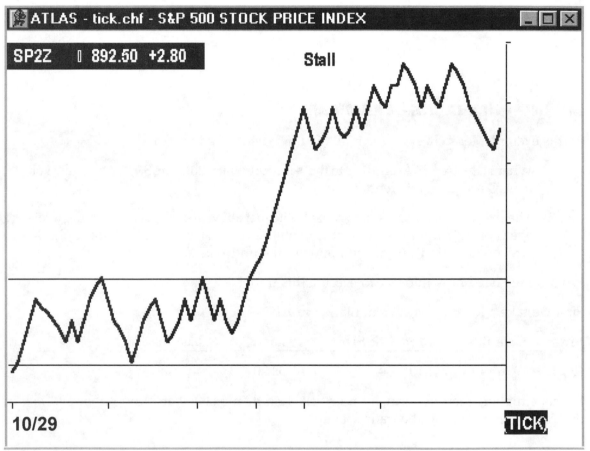

Figure 14-14

BUYING PULLBACKS—EXAMPLE 3

In this example, let's check to see if all the ingredients are in place:

☑ What is the trend? According to the 1-minute chart, both the S&P futures as well as AIG are in an up-trend.

☑ The price action has begun to consolidate just above the 20-period moving average (Point X) and the stochastics are on the verge of crossing back up (Point X) which would indicate a resumption of the up-trend.

What do we need now in order to execute this trade?

First we take a look at the current market in AIG:

Bid	Ask	Bid/Ask Size	Last	Last Size
62.25	62.40	10 × 30	62.30	40

In this situation there is virtually no stock (less than 5,000 shares) on either side, so in this case I will pay up if the trade sets up.

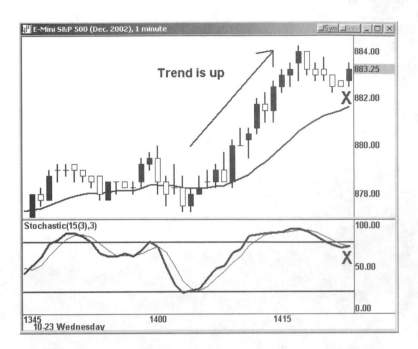

Figure 14-15

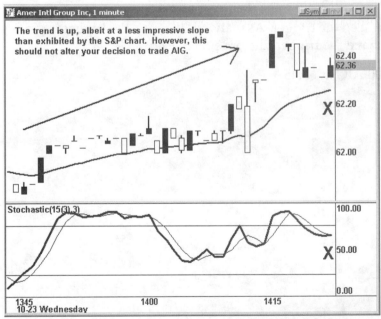

Figure 14-16

☑ Now we need the trigger. As is always the case, the trigger is the tick chart. Now that we have the trigger, the order is placed:

☑ Buy 1,000 AIG at 62.45.

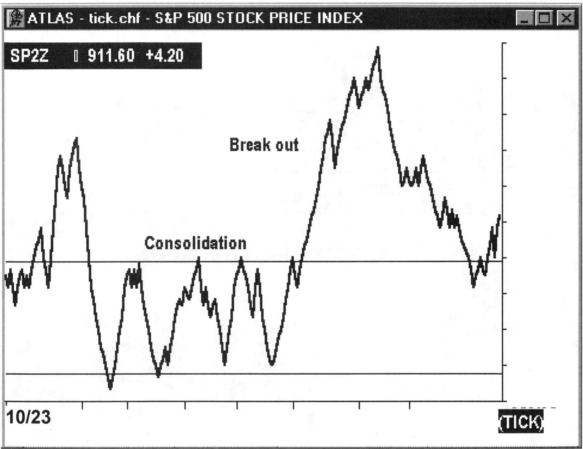

Figure 14-17

Thomson Financial

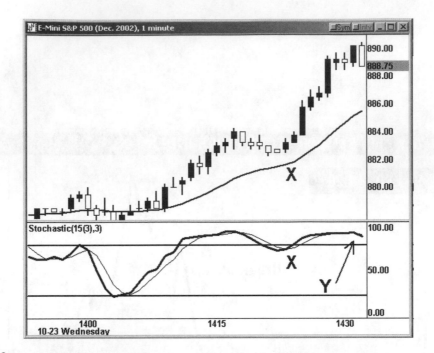

Figure 14-18

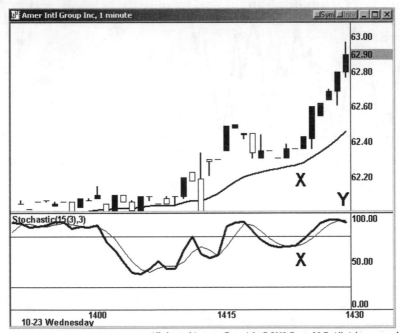

Figure 14-19

I was filled at 62.40, the trade played out as follows:

You will notice that in this trade the S&P move is very quick and decisive. It quickly goes from 884 to almost 889 without a pause. In this case, the limitations of stochastics become evident.

When stochastics become overbought/oversold, it may, under certain circumstances, simply indicate a powerful trend. This can last several bars. Rather than try to guess whether or not this is in fact one of those rare occasions, continue to use the tick chart as your guide for exits. You are better off capturing the meat of the move than trying to sell the absolute top print. My experience has always been that it is better to play the odds.

In this case, once the S&Ps reach 886, they appear that they are about to cross back down, yet the price action continues higher for several more bars.

☑ Once the stochastics indicate that turn is imminent (Point Y) as well as the pause in the tick chart (see below), you need to exit the trade.

☑ Sell 1,000 AIG at Market. I was filled at 62.70.

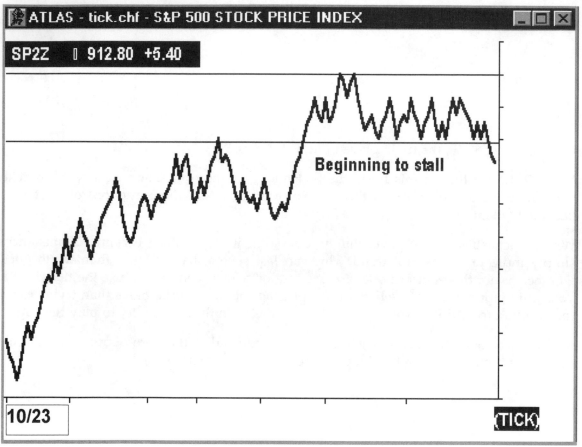

Figure 14-20

Thomson Financial

If I had waited, a sell-off followed shortly thereafter.

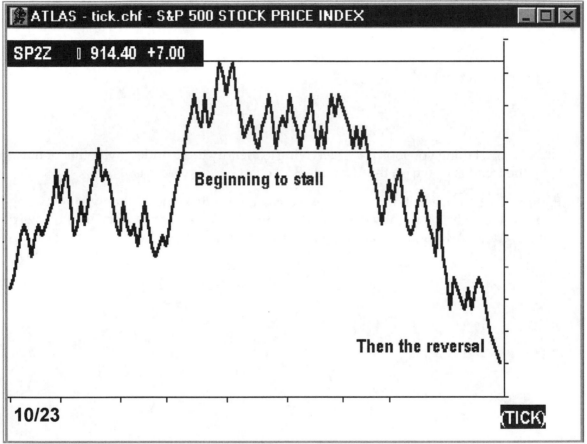

Figure 14-21

Thomson Financial

SHORT SELLING RALLIES—EXAMPLE 1

Short selling rallies are really just the opposite of buying pullbacks. Personally, these are my favorite trades.

Call me a perma-bear if you like, but it has also been statistically proven that stocks go down faster than they go up. Let's walk through an example.

☑ The first thing you look for when trying to identify these trades is whether or not the trend is down on the 1-minute S&P chart, in this case it is.

In Figure 14-22, notice at Point X we have a change in the slope of the moving average, from up to the right, to slightly down and to the left, as well as the price bars below the moving average. Additionally, the stochastics are pointing down.

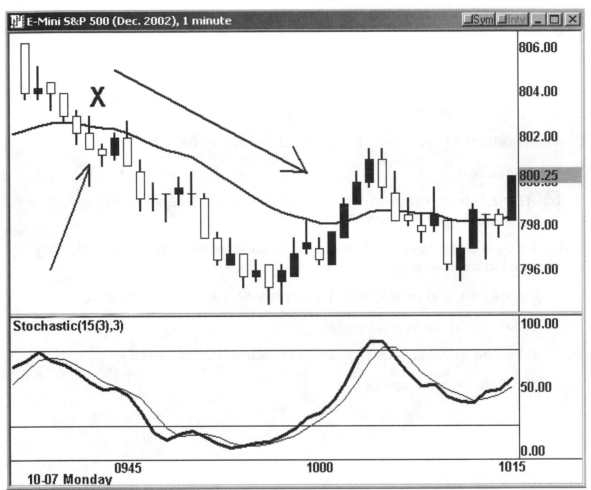

Figure 14-22

Once the stochastics have moved into oversold territory at Point Y:

You will notice that:

☑ The S&Ps begin to consolidate as noted by the A and B channels and the stochastic begins to turn back up (Points Y to Z).

It is not required that they reach back into the neutral territory (above 20). They just have to reset in some way.

This is exactly what you need to train your eyes to see, the trade is setting up.

1. A downtrend has been identified.

2. Prices are pausing, potentially about to resume the downtrend.

3. The stochastics are resetting.

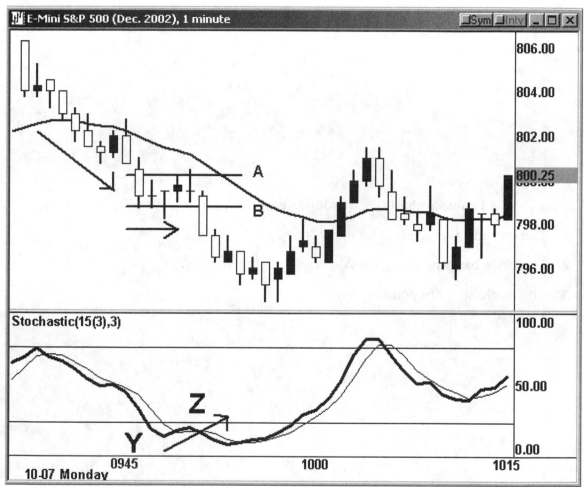

Figure 14-23

Here we have a 1-minute chart of Citigroup. Again, as noted by Point X:

1. The moving average is sloping down.

2. The price bars are below the 20-period moving average.

3. The stochastics are pointing down.

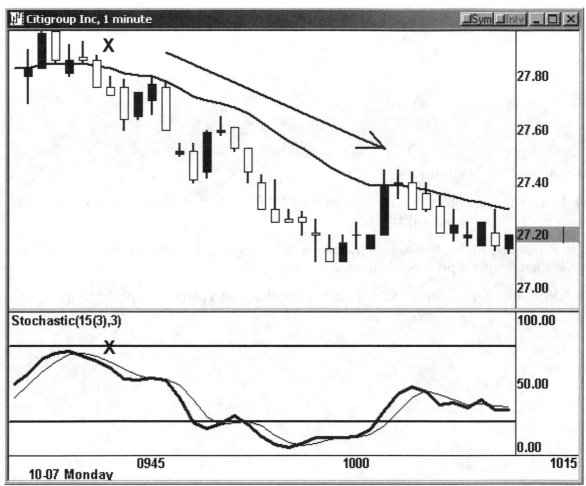

Figure 14-24

Fast-forward a few minutes:

While the chart is not an exact replica of the S&P futures, it is close enough to serve the needs of establishing a short trade.

In this instance, the A/B channels indicate a move back up towards the moving average rather than simply a price consolidation.

The stochastics are resetting at Points Y-Z. Everything is in place, except the trigger.

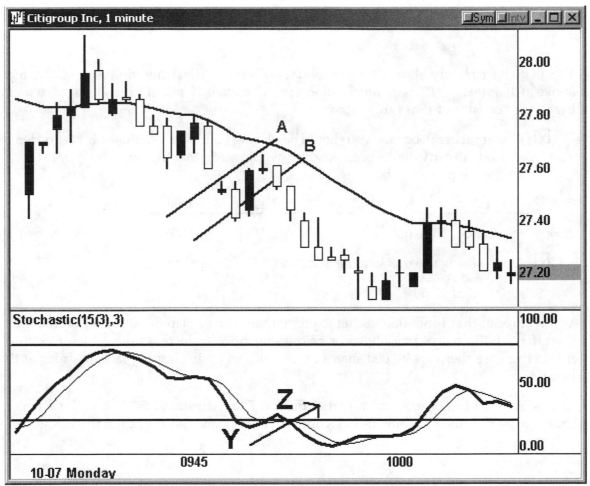

Figure 14-25

The tick chart clearly shows the consolidation seen in the 1-minute chart of the S&Ps above (Channels A/B) but, **more importantly, makes it much clearer as to when a break (or "burst") of that range occurs.**

☑ Once that break occurs, you should be placing your trade. At this point the order should already have been loaded, waiting for the trigger. The market in Citigroup presently is:

Bid	Ask	Bid/Ask Size	Last	Last Size
27.50	27.55	100 × 30	27.53	500

☑ Upon seeing the break in the tick chart, I immediately send my order:

Sell 2,000 C at 27.50

You will recall that I mentioned that anytime there is less than 5,000 shares on the bid or the offer, I will always pay above or below that price to increase the odds of getting a fill. In this case there are 10,000 shares on the bid, so I will simply place an order at that price.

In this instance I only received a partial fill of 1,700 shares at 27.50. When the other 300 shares were not filled within 10–15 seconds, I simply canceled the remaining order.

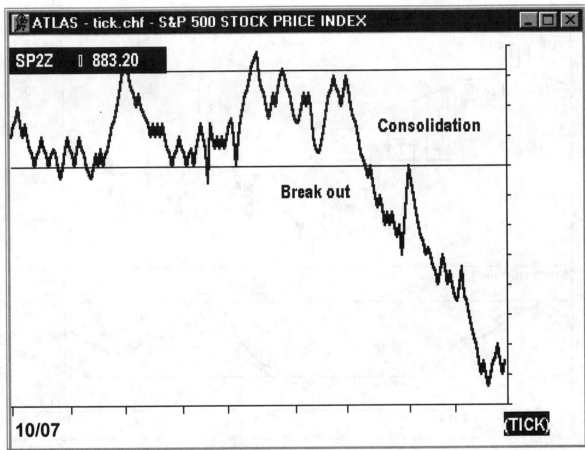

Figure 14-26

So let's see how the trade played out.

The S&Ps broke hard and fast out of that consolidation channel (Point X) . . .

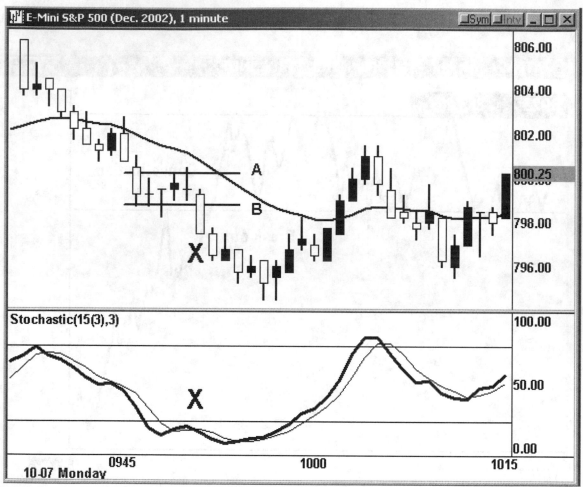

Figure 14-27

. . . as did Citigroup

So with the S&Ps at my back, I simply focus on the price action in Citigroup and the tick chart for exit clues.

The market in Citigroup is now (Point X):

Bid	Ask	Bid/Ask Size	Last	Last Size
27.45	27.50	10 × 80	27.50	900

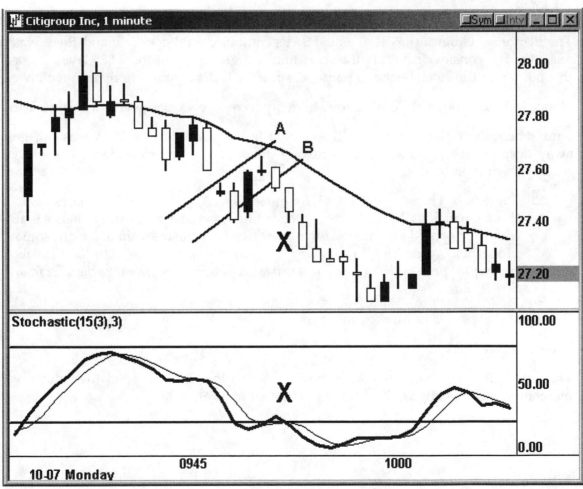

Figure 14-28

☑ Next I watch for the downward momentum to slow.

The market in Citigroup as well as the S&Ps continued to deteriorate and there was no reason yet to consider covering the short until Citigroup got to the 27.25 level. It was at this point that the stock began to pause, despite the S&Ps continuing their move lower.

Notice in Figure 14-29 at Point A you suddenly have sideways movement for two bars.

Simultaneously, I also notice that the current bid in Citigroup of 27.25 was not going away despite several large trades occurring there whose total exceeded what was currently showing on the bid.

☑ These two "clues" were enough for me to cover 1,000 of the 1,700 shares I was short. Given that the S&Ps were still heading lower, there was still a chance that Citigroup would resume its downward trend. In the meantime, lock in some profits just in case. *This is a case where I reduced my exposure independently of a weakening of the tick. As time goes by, you will learn how to deviate from the checklist from time to time.*

Buy 1,000 shares of C at Market

I was filled at 27.32

The remaining 700 shares would be covered when the S&Ps stopped their downward momentum or the Citigroup continued to find support at 27.25.

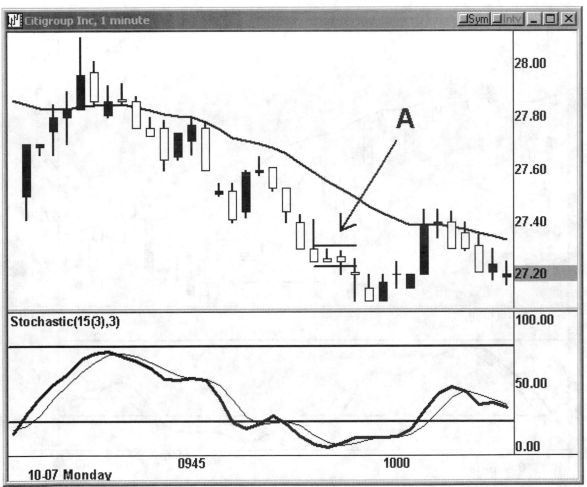

Figure 14-29

Eventually the 27.25 level did give way on Citigroup and trades lower as seen in Point A on the chart below.

☑ But with the stochastics beginning to turn back up (Point Y) and . . .

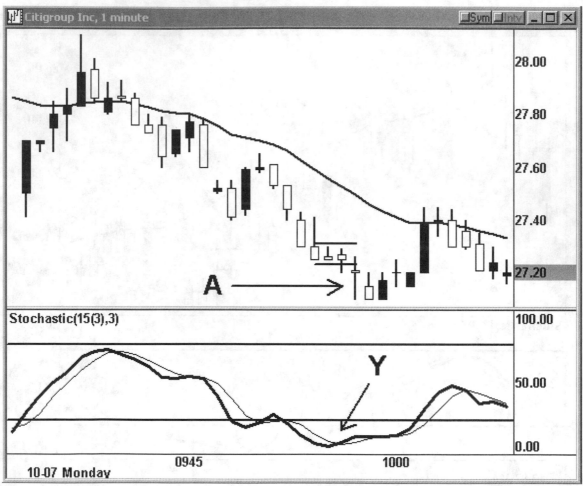

Figure 14-30

☑ . . . the tick chart showing some signs of consolidation (Point X), it was time to cover the remaining 700 shares.

☑ Buy 700 shares of C at Market!

I was filled at 27.15.

Staying in the extra time while locking in a profit, allowed me to maximize the trade. Yes, there will be many times when getting out all at once would have been the better alternative, but it is impossible to know.

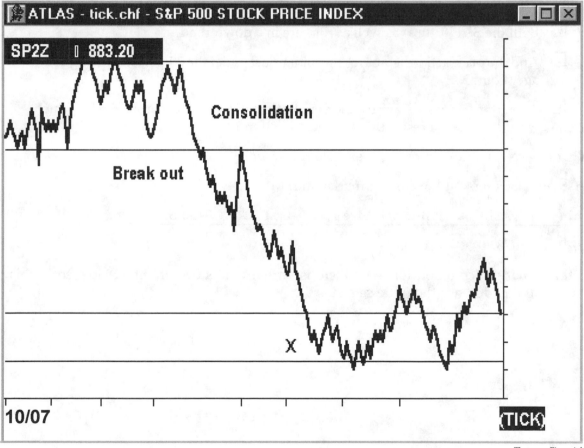

Thomson Financial

Figure 14-31

SHORT SELLING RALLIES—EXAMPLE 2

In this example we have a situation where:

☑ Both the S&P futures as well as IBM are in a downtrend.

☑ And the price action begins to consolidate just under the 20-period moving average (Point X).

☑ Also, the stochastics are on the verge of crossing back down (Point X) which would indicate a resumption of the downtrend.

What do we need now in order to execute this trade?

First we take a look at the current market in IBM:

Bid	Ask	Bid/Ask Size	Last	Last Size
78.70	78.80	1 × 1	78.75	500

In this situation (common for IBM) there is virtually no stock on either side, so in this case I will pay down if the trade sets up.

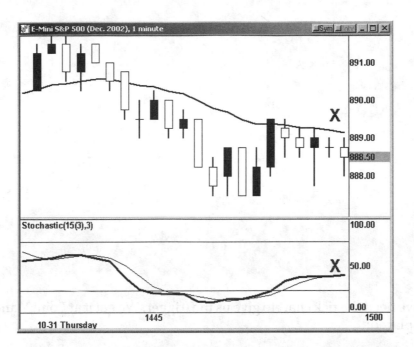

Figure 14-32

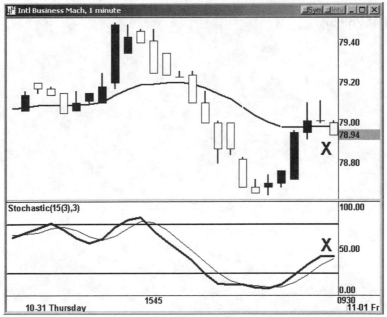

Figure 14-33

☑ Now we need the tick chart to give us the trigger. We get it at Point Y and the order is placed:

☑ **Sell 1,000 IBM at 78.65**

I was filled at 78.65.

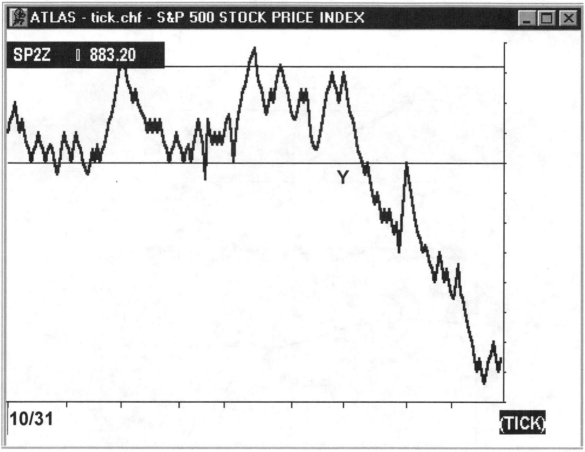

Figure 14-34

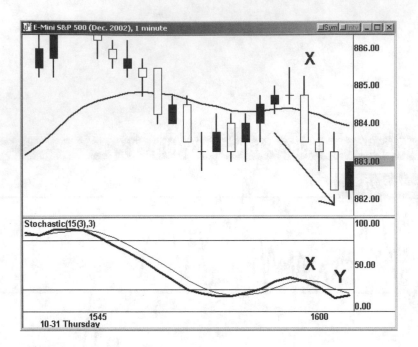

Figure 14-35

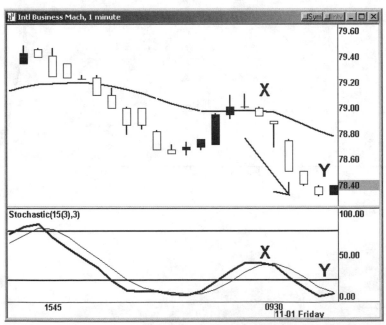

Figure 14-36

The trade played out as shown. You will notice that in this trade the S&P move is very short in duration, just a bit over 3 points as well as about 3 minutes in terms of time.

☑ Once the stochastics indicate that a turn is imminent (Point Y) . . .

☑ . . . as well as the pause in the tick chart at B (see below), you need to exit the trade.

There is no room for argument or rationalization. It is what it is. The trade is over:

☑ Buy 1,000 IBM at Market

I was filled at 78.40.

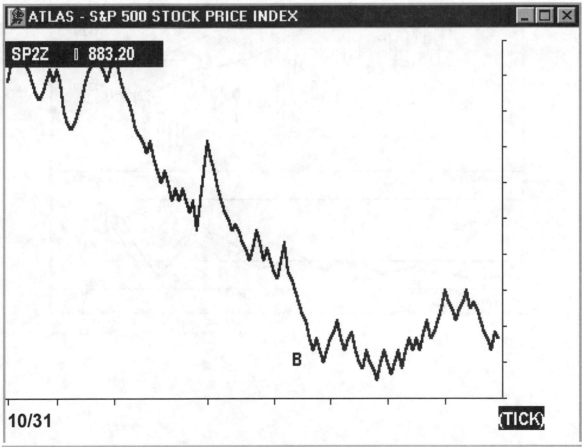

Figure 14-37

SHORT SELLING RALLIES—EXAMPLE 3

The following example is another trade in IBM. It is very similar to the previous one and just goes to show once again that HVT traders are creatures of habit. That is the way I trade and I suggest you do the same.

Figure 14-38

Figure 14-39

☑ Here again, you see that both the S&P futures as well as IBM are in a downtrend.

☑ There is a minor rally off that downtrend.

☑ Next, the price action begins to consolidate just under the 20-period moving average (Point X) and the stochastics are on the verge of crossing back down (Point X). This suggests to me that a resumption of the downtrend is at hand.

What do we need now in order to execute this trade?

First we take a look at the current market in IBM:

Bid	Ask	Bid/Ask Size	Last	Last Size
82.60	82.70	10 × 3	82.63	10

In this situation, just like the previous one, there is virtually no stock on either side, so in this case I will pay down if the trade sets up.

☑ Now we need the trigger. As is always the case, the trigger is the tick chart. Note the breakdown at Point A.

☑ Now that we have the trigger, the order is placed: Sell 1,000 IBM at 82.55.

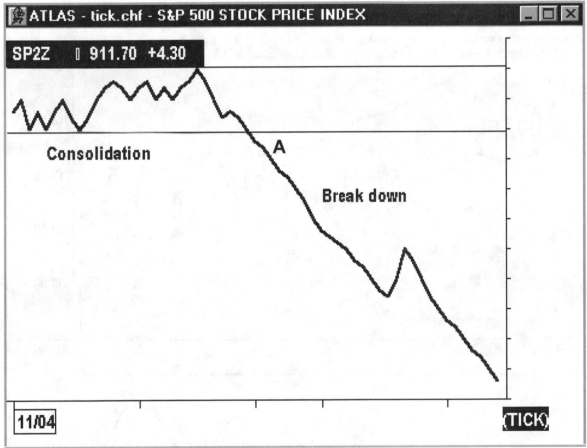

Figure 14-40

I was filled at 82.58, the trade played out as follows:

Like the previous trade I showed you, the S&P move is very short in duration, just a bit over 3 points as well as about 3 minutes in terms of time.

☑ Once the stochastics indicate that turn is imminent (Point Y) as well as the pause in the tick chart (Point Z), you need to exit the trade.

☑ Buy 1,000 IBM at Market. I was filled at 82.37.

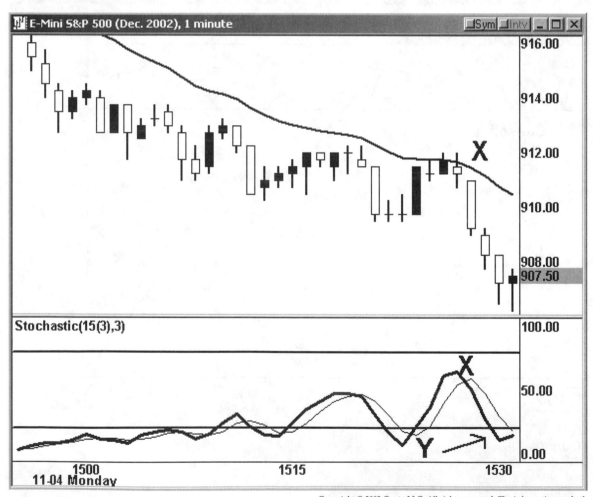

Figure 14-41

CHAPTER 14

Figure 14-42

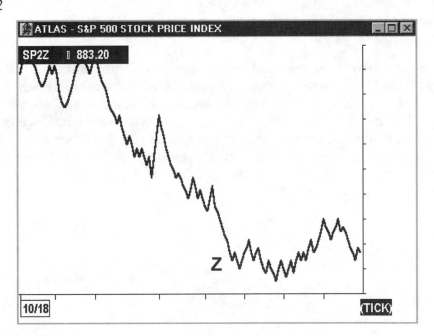

Figure 14-43

Now . . . what if I had decided to get greedy?

Let's just say for the sake of illustration that I decided to break my own rules and hang on for another move down. This is what would have happened:

> The stochastics crossed back (Point Y) up and within 2 minutes the S&Ps were back near the area you initiated the short position from.

> Given that IBM is so closely correlated with the S&P futures, you can almost guarantee it will have rallied back as well. Sure enough, IBM rallied all the way back to the entry price.

In HVT, you will often see moves go beyond your exit point. In other words, if you had hung to a position longer, you theoretically could have made more money. That is something that you must learn to watch with no regret whatsoever. HVT focuses on the portion of any given move in which the probability of success is high. Once our indicators are telling us that that is no longer the case, the trade goes from being a walk across the street on a green light to becoming the more risky proposition of running across the Interstate 10 during rush hour, blindfolded. Yes, you might get away with it a few times, but I really don't think you can make a living that way.

Figure 14-44

Figure 14-45

CHAPTER FIFTEEN

Your HVT Trading Plan

> The title of this chapter sounds like I'm talking about life insurance. But that's what money management and trading psychology are . . .

Nothing I teach you in this book will do you any good unless it all rests on the foundation of following sane guidelines that will help you avoid catastrophe and maximize success. Here are my recommendations.

1. **Start off trading 100 shares at a time until you can consistently net $100 per day or more, for a period of two weeks.** After that, follow the same approach with 200 shares . . . $200, 400 shares . . . $400 etc.

2. **Always define your stop loss.** In Chapter 8, I explained how I normally exit trades using tick charts. However, I always, always define a stop as an insurance policy. Very rarely do I get stopped out, because I usually exit a trade manually. But using a stop assures that if the market goes against you, it won't be a catastrophe. I think a good rule of thumb is to set your stop at 5 to 10 cents. However, if the market and the stock you are trading are not going in the direction you thought, just get out of the trade. There is no need for your stop

loss to be hit. (Given the frequency and duration of the trades, stops need to be mental, physical stops are just not possible.)

3. **Get to know a handful of stocks, preferably one or two from the major sectors like Technology, Drugs, Biotech, Energy, etc., and trade only those stocks.** Each stock has a personality, simply due to the fact that it is the same specialist or market maker every day. Human beings are creatures of habit and they always repeat their habits. The better you know how the Merrill Lynch market maker or, say, the IBM specialist handles certain situations, the better off you will be. It is one more edge you give yourself over everyone else.

4. **Let the market/trades come to you.** Never trade for excitement, and try not to trade during the mid-morning session (11:30 A.M. to 2:00 P.M. EST).

5. **Keep opinions to a minimum.** The trades should be based on what you see and not what you think will happen. However, with time, you will develop a keen insight which is intangible, and must be trusted and implemented into your plan.

6. **Stick with it.** Too many people, perhaps even some who purchased this book, stick with the plan and don't execute it correctly. They become disappointed. They then go on to the next approach, never developing consistency. Make no mistake, this will take a lot of time and effort to master. I tell all new traders who come into my office to expect very little in the way of income the first few months. As you can already tell, HVT when all is said and done is still more of an art than a science. The science part is the chart patterns which help you identify potential entry and exit points. The rest is your "feel" (not opinion) for the market at any given point in time. This will only come with experience.

DEVELOPING THE MENTAL DISCIPLINE TO FOLLOW YOUR STOPS WITHOUT FAIL

Placing stop loss orders is real simple in HVT, provided you have the right mindset. Ask yourself one simple question:

Is the market, at this very moment, still moving in the direction I had anticipated just a few minutes ago?

If it is, consider staying in the trade. If not, you need to exit the trade, or in some circumstances maybe get out of half of the position.

Remember the reason you got into the trade? The S&Ps were either bursting up or down. So, if they are not moving in that direction any longer, why stay in? Secondly, since the stock you are trading is closely correlated with the S&Ps, you can be reasonably sure that the stock will stop moving in that direction also.

I used to work with a trader who I still think about to this day. He was a true realist when it came to trading. He never tried to outguess the market. He just simply traded what he saw. I suspect he learned this from his blackjack days in Vegas. If you are playing cards and your hand is terrible, like a 3 and a 5 card, you cannot argue with yourself that they are 2 face cards.

You can't explain it away; why should a trade be any different?

This same trader had a great way of illustrating the absurdity of rationalizing away bad trades:

> If someone throws a brick at you, and it is coming right for your head, you don't sit there and say:
>
> "Gee, I wonder if that brick will hit my head?"
>
> No, you duck to avoid being hit. A bad trade or a trade that is no longer valid is no different.

I believe the big difference between the brick example and the bad trade example can be explained by the way our brains are wired. Most of us attach a stigma to being wrong in trading. There is no shame in jumping out of the way of a brick, but there appears to be an unwillingness to jump out of harm's way when it involves money. This is for each individual to come to terms with. I suggest you think long and hard about this if you have this tendency. Refer to some of the work done by Mark Douglas—you will find it helpful.

THE CHOICE IS YOURS

I want to provide you with the trading knowledge that will give you the best possible odds for succeeding in this business. However, there are still some variables that I cannot control.

Your personality will play a key role in whether or not you succeed as a HVT trader. If you are not perfectly suited for trading, then you will have to make a supreme effort to change. It is highly beneficial for you to know where you stand ahead of the game. Give this some serious thought. While trading is intense on all levels, I personally feel it is several notches higher when you trade on the time frames that are taught here.

Still interested? Great. Then let me ask you a few questions. These are the same questions I ask all new traders that express an interest in trading with my firm, Aspen Trading Group, Inc. Over the years I have developed a pretty solid understanding of what a person's mindset and attitude need to be, in order for them to have a better-than-average chance at succeeding. The answers are by no means an absolute measure, but offer some insight. Ultimately the decision will be made by you, not me or TradingMarkets, so be honest with yourself.

1. Do you have at least six months to a year of living expenses set aside to assist you while you start your new trading business?

2. What similarities or differences do you see between trading and playing blackjack or poker?

3. Are you overly emotional? Do you become overly euphoric or disappointed by winning and losing trades?

4. Do you believe that trading is a game where it is you vs. the market?

5. Why do you feel you would be a great HVT trader?

Ponder over these questions seriously. Write your answers on a sheet of paper. And be honest. Once you have done this. Turn to the next page.

1. Do you have at least six months to a year of living expenses set aside to assist you while you start your new trading business?

   When I teach you my trading techniques, you may think that you can learn them in a couple of weeks. That may be true. But the polished skill that you need in order to apply them properly takes a great deal of time and hands-on live trading to develop. I know this from my own experience as well as observing those whom I have personally taught. **Don't be cocky.** I have seen people who think they know it all, completely blow out within a month. **You must allow yourself an adequate amount of time to successfully climb the learning curve.**

2. What similarities or differences do you see between trading and playing blackjack or poker?

   I ask this question as a way of getting you to cough up a response that reveals whether you will approach trading as though you are playing slot machines in a Las Vegas casino or if you view this as a game of skill in which your moment-by-moment decisions have a direct impact on how much money you make each day. **Each and every trade you make must be treated as an intelligent business decision that is structured to make profits.**

3. Are you overly emotional? Do you become overly euphoric or disappointed by winning and losing trades?

   Properly executed individual trades, whether they are wins or losses, are the stepping-stones to weekly, monthly, and yearly profits. To trade successfully, you need keep your emotions under control at all times. You cannot allow any one trade to cause you to get so emotional that it affects your judgment on the next trade. Doing so is a prescription for failure.

4. Do you believe that trading is a game where it is you vs. the market?

   If there is one thing that is certain, it is that if you ever try to fight the market, the market will always, always, always win. There is zero probability that your desire or will has any effect on what the market does. The market simply does not care about what you and I think. **The key to being a profitable trader is to follow what the market does and trade in sync with it.** And in those cases where you can't, don't trade.

5. Why do you feel you would be a great HVT trader?

There are answers you could give me that would tell me that you really need to rethink whether you are suited for trading. Here are some of them:

a. I have been successful in another professional career outside of trading.

b. I have a burning desire to make a lot of money in a short period of time.

c. I think trading would be easy for me to learn.

d. I am about to get laid off and I want to quickly start a new career as a full-time professional trader.

e. I am an engineer and trading is no more difficult than any other problem I have ever solved.

On the other hand, if your answers are more along these lines, then I would say that you've got the potential to be a successful HVT trader:

a. **I want to succeed and *I will follow your trading rules* to the best of my abilities.**

b. **I see trading as a game and I want to learn and apply *a strategy that will put the odds in my favor.***

c. **I realize that while I can make money, I can also lose it all too. Therefore, I'm going to make sure that I *protect myself on every trade I make.***

d. **I have no ego going into this thing. *I realize that I will have to admit I'm wrong on a regular basis.***

e. **I realize this is a difficult profession to master, but I'm going be patient and take it slow . . . one day at a time . . . *and learn continuously from my mistakes.***

The views I express above about the character and makeup of successful traders are not based on opinion. They are based on my observation of many dozens of traders that I have personally trained and mentored. Over time, I have been able to accurately assess the probability that a trainee would succeed, based upon how they answered these questions.

So then—how did your answers compare to the ones that I consider to be appropriate? If you noticed that your thought process is similar to mine, then I encourage you to dive right into HVT trading. However, if your answers tended to deviate from the answers I provided, then you have to attack the business of trading successfully on multiple fronts. Please be sure to use the resources relating to discipline, money management and trading psychology provided at the back of this book.

ANOTHER EXIT TECHNIQUE: TAKING TIME OFF

Too often as traders, we fear that we will miss great trading opportunities if we do not show up each and every day. While that may be true, I look at it this way: When I am not trading well, I start to miss trades and not see great trade setups that normally I would pounce on. Secondly, I start to become very apprehensive about my entry points and frequently get in too late, rather than being "mechanized" to simply react and go for the throat on my entry and exit points. In short, if I am not trading well, the markets could be very volatile (great for daytrading), yet it won't benefit me in any way, since I am less than 100%.

The key for newer traders is recognizing when you are experiencing this and having the ability to get up and walk away for a few days.

How does a new trader identify these periods without confusing them with just laziness or an excuse to take a vacation? I suppose the answer will be different for each person, but I feel that there are certain signs that are probably quite common among all traders:

1. Noticing that your performance is suffering

2. Missing trades that you normally would take

3. Hesitating on entry points, in short, "over-thinking" the trade (paralysis by analysis)

4. When you get up in the morning do you have that "eye of the tiger" and supreme confidence?

Remember that there is no reason to feel bad about experiencing any of these moods or symptoms, which are normal for traders. Traders are under so much stress and operate at such heightened states of awareness longer than most people do in a day, that their bodies just can't sustain it after a while. Joe DiNaploi, of DiNapoli Levels and Fibonacci numbers fame, suggests that traders take a week off every two to three months. You will be surprised at how refreshed you are when you get back. More importantly, your clarity will be back, enabling you to once again see the nuances and subtleties that allowed your trading to excel in the first place.

One other aspect to keep in mind is distractions. It is so easy to get sidetracked by the phone, other people, etc. Put yourself in an environment where you can isolate yourself from these distractions.

FINAL THOUGHTS

I have thrown a tremendous amount of material at you in this book. I expect that you will need to revisit it several times before you can actually begin to use it to its true potential. I am working on additional material and services to complement your understanding of HVT.

In the meantime, set your goals, focus and by all means remain disciplined. If you start with those three, you are well on your way. This quote applies:

> If you have set your goals and are working towards them each and every day, there is no reason to be discouraged by minor setbacks, for whoever continues to pursue that goal with intensity and desire, the goal cannot help but be attained.

—Anonymous

Good luck and good trading,

David Floyd

APPENDIX

About the Author

David Floyd is a professional daytrader and President of Aspen Trading Group. He trades highly liquid NYSE stocks and makes between 25 and 100 trades each day. His strategy, which incorporates market dynamics, patterns and momentum, has allowed him to achieve returns of 428% for 1998, 668% for 1999, 1132% for 2000, and 208% in 2001, and 262% in 2002. David is married with a son and lives in Southern California where his hobbies include boating and European soccer.

NOTES:

NOTES:

NOTES:

NOTES:

NOTES:

NOTES: